VISUALISATION TO REALISATION

By
Jackie Carroll
&
Lloyd Chambers

Copyright © 2018 Jackie Carroll & Lloyd Chambers

All rights reserved.

This book is designed to provide information and motivation to our readers. It is sold with the understanding that the publisher is not engaged to render any type of psychological, legal, or any other kind of professional advice. No warranties or guarantees are expressed or implied. Neither the publisher nor the individual author(s) shall be liable for any physical, psychological, emotional, financial, or commercial damages, including, but not limited to, special, incidental, consequential, or other damages. Our views and rights are the same: You are responsible for your own choices, actions, and results.

ISBN-13: 978-1986608183

ISBN-10: 1986608182

First Printing June 2018

CONTENTS

FOREWORD BY BOB PROCTOR 1
CHAPTER 1: GENIE... 3
   Jackie's Story: A Mom Inventor's Story 3
   Lloyd's Story: An Old Soul's Journey 7
CHAPTER 2: WHAT IS HOLDING YOU BACK...................... 13
CHAPTER 3: THEY MADE ME DO IT, THOSE NASTY
   GREMLINS 33
   Gremlin N°1: Poor Self-Image 33
   Gremlin N°2: Lack of Faith... 38
   Gremlin N°3: Belief in the Bigger Picture......................39
   333 Story by Bob Proctor 41
   Gremlin N°4: Following Through/ Staying the Course 46
CHAPTER 4: I AM SO GRATEFUL I KNOW THOSE LAWS .. 55
   How to Use Future Gratitude... 57
   Your Why, Your What, and Your How 58
   The 7 Hermetic Laws of Ancient Kemet........................ 61
CHAPTER 5: HIGHER WHAT?...65
   Mind Work 66
CHAPTER 6: REPEAT, REPEAT, REPEAT & LOVE THAT
   MIRROR...83
CHAPTER 7: GETTING ALL SCIENTIFIC IN HERE.............. 91
   Emotion and Intuition.. 91
CHAPTER 8: LIVING IN THE CLOUDS 103
   The Importance of Making Decisions 104
   The Principle of Agreed Imagined Reality 107
CHAPTER 9: BECOMING MAGNETIC................................... 111
   Peggy McColl 111
   Claudia DeVries 121
   Monica DaMaren 127
   Ewa Pietrzak 129

Foreword by Bob Proctor

You've made an excellent decision by reading Jackie and Lloyd's book. *Visualisation to Realisation* is rich with stories, valuable information, and strategies to show you steps that others have taken and you must take if you really want to live the life you desire.

Visualization is one of the most important things you can do if you want more from life. We have been gifted with Higher Faculties: Memory, Reason, Intuition, Perception, Will, and Imagination.

We need to practice Will to be able to hold an image on the screen of our mind to the exclusion of outside distraction, and Imagination to make that image come to life. It's an excellent method for helping you attract the good you desire — in all areas of your life.

Most people don't know their life purpose, and don't have clearly defined goals, so it's no wonder they don't have a vision.

Your purpose explains what you are doing with your life. Your vision explains how you are living your purpose. Your goals enable you to realize your vision. Once you have these in place, this is where you can use the art of visualization.

All the great achievers from the past have been visionary figures; they were men and women who saw into the future. They thought of what could be, rather than what already was, and then they moved themselves into action to bring these things to fruition.

The information in this book is enormously valuable; read it and apply it. Throughout these chapters you'll discover how your vision is invaluable in the process to success in life. If you can conceive it in your mind, you certainly can hold it in your hand. The beautifully talented people who share their stories in this book are ordinary people like you and I, achieving extraordinary things in life, and if they can do it, so can you.

Jackie and Lloyd both have been mentored at the Proctor Gallagher Institute through our *Thinking into Results* program — an in-depth 12-step process to a life of abundance and fulfilled desire. They embody the very principles we teach. I had the pleasure of meeting Jackie at the Matrixx in April 2017 and 2018. Watching her vision become her reality, it is a true testament to Earl Nightingale's definition of success: "Success is the progressive realization of a worthy ideal."

You see, this is the thing. All of us ordinary people are only one step away from being extraordinary contributors to this thing we call life. We are all talented creative individuals with more talent and ability tied up in our spiritual DNA than we could ever imagine.

The purpose of this book is to share the tools of how ordinary people like you and me — and just like Jackie and Lloyd — can achieve tremendous things with the application of belief and visualization and the Universal Laws. You see, the process of Visualizing is truly the key to manifesting anything you desire in your life.

As you read, you will discover that it's now your turn to open up the pages to your own success story of abundance and prosperity in all the areas of your life!

    Bob Proctor,

    New York Times Best Selling Author,
    Motivational Speaker & Personal Development Leader

Chapter 1: Genie

Jackie's Story: A Mom Inventor's Story

My Teen Years – When My Entrepreneurial Mind Awoke

I was born in Zimbabwe, grew up in South Africa, and now live in Ireland with my beautiful family. I am a mom to three beautiful children, 4 fur babies, and wife to my best friend.

I have wanted to own my own business since I was a teenager. My dad worked for a company for 15 years. He gave his life to this company. He was at work more than he was home.

One day, out of the blue, my dad was made redundant.

Looking back now, I'm sure it was because of his age, as the company wanted to bring in fresh blood. But at my tender age, I couldn't understand how he could have devoted so much of his life to this company — only for them to toss him out.

That day had a huge effect on me. I didn't want that to ever happen to me. I wanted to be able to spend time with my family and still be financially secure. I saw myself in the future wearing a fancy suit and carrying a fancy briefcase.

My College Years – When My Heart Was Broken

I finished school and went to college. In 1998, when I was 19 years old, my Mom died of ovarian cancer. She was only 54, and far too young to die.

My mom had the most amazing energy, and people wanted to be around her all the time. She listened intently when people spoke. Her caring for others, as well as the world around her, was more than apparent. People were attracted to my mom and her magnetic joy in life.

Which was why her death was so heartbreaking.

I watched my Mom die unhappy.

She had given up on her dreams and hope had abandoned her.

My Move to Ireland – Healing the Heart and Mind

I moved to Ireland in 2003 and soon met my future husband. We enjoyed life together, traveling around until our two smallest babies began to grow bigger. My husband had his own successful business and now I wanted a stab at it. I wanted a project of my own.

Not wanting to take on a lot of risk and with the goal to up my confidence a bit, I invested time and money into a home-based business. I was up and down and all over the show, selling and recruiting and running seminars.

Until I finally gave in to what I was being told: that I should be working 9–5. It's amazing how life can throw you a few curve balls — great learning curve balls I might add. That was exactly what I needed to get out of the house and focus my time and energy on my own self-development journey.

I soon bore witness to how the universe guides you to where you need to be and people you need in your life at different moments in time.

My Lightbulb Moment

I signed up for a program called *Thinking Into Results* created by Bob Proctor and Sandy Gallagher and taught by my one and only beautiful coach and mentor, Ewa Pietrzak. I did the course twice.

This is important, as it was the *second time around* when I had my lightbulb moment. The concept of *Genie in a Headset* was conceived.

In 2016 when I put pen to paper, oh man, did it feel right.

I was going to Create a Virtual Reality Vision Board.

I saw in my mind a game where people could create their visions and their dreams in virtual reality and then actually experience it.

This made so much sense to me. And then the neg ferrets came out...

Funny thing is — this whole self-development malarkey teaches you to trust your gut. And like windscreen wipers flicking bugs off the car window... I was able to block out all the negative background noise and hear only, go for it... *just go for it.*

Who cares what people are saying?

Who cares that it doesn't make sense to them?

So I did: I went for it. I pitched myself on *VOOM*, on weekend start-ups. I talked and talked to so many people, building energy behind my idea. And then by pure guidance, I live-streamed Bob and Sandy's *Paradigm Shift* seminar. I saw their video advertisement for *The Matrixx* event and by April 2017 I was in Toronto shaking hands with Bob and Sandy.

When My Dream Started Becoming Reality

By the end of June 2017, I had secured 3 investors and GIAH International was born.

My dream was now a reality!

Jackie's Life Purpose

I knew I wanted to help people with visualization.

I want to make it the simplest possible way so that even kids could understand how to do it.

I have children and they are the future: I want to give them really good things for their future.

That's why I get really excited when I hear about kids and teenagers and other young people thinking about self-development.

When my mom passed, I had the thought then that I didn't want people to die thinking that life was just misery until it ended.

I don't want that!

I want to help facilitate the reality that life is what you make it, and any way you want it to be. I want people to love their life and make it awesome. I don't want people dying without being able to do that. Life is pretty epic! If you teach kids, and young adults and teenagers that they have the power to live a glorious life… I think the world might be a bigger, brighter, and more beautiful place.

What YOU Can Learn from ME

I believe that regardless of any situation for people there are two things that are vitally important:

Your Dreams and Hopes. If you take those away what do you have?

I don't care if people say, "Dreams aren't reality." I totally disagree. Let's chat about it sometime over a latté… or champagne, whichever you prefer.

Live with hope in your heart, dreams in your head, and a smile on your face, and you have a lot more than most!

I don't want people feeling like their dreams aren't important. I don't want people to live without hope.

This, my beautiful people, is what my life purpose is, what GIAH International values and why we call ourselves the crusaders of your dreams!

We are here to fight for your dreams, to give you hope, and to make you fall in love with life all over again!

You have only one shot at it, better make sure it's a damn good one and don't let anyone take that away from you, *ESPECIALLY* yourself!!

I want to invite you to join our community of like-minded people who are on a journey that starts in the imagination and ends in creation. This journey begins with your dreams being visualized and ends with your dreams becoming reality.

I want to invite you to a community where your dreams matter, and your visions count!

Whether you're after:

- a journey of self-discovery
- a course to help you get what you want, or
- maybe to learn what you want
- an accountability partner, or
- an exciting game in Virtual Reality that truly is the portal to a life you dream of!

GIAH is all of that!

Having your own personal Genie has its advantages, as you will see!

Lloyd's Story: An Old Soul's Journey

My earliest memory is lying on the grass and watching the summer clouds pass overhead. As I wondered what filled the space between as the particles of pollen floated by on the breeze, I set out on a journey that has led me into a deep understanding of the human condition and how we relate to the world around us.

Two years later while stuck in a boarding school to keep me out of trouble, I was woken by a gentle shake to the shoulder. There was some news, I was told. The trip down to the phone through that old building seemed long and cold, but it was nothing compared to the journey back to bed after hearing the news.

My grandmother had passed away.

It was the first and last time I cried for many years. This was not to be the last time I witnessed death, of course. As people disappeared from my world, it seemed clear to me that there had to be a point to the life and death process.

There had to be a job to do during the transition from birth to death and back again.

From an early age, I was a very deep thinker. I was more interested in the reason why things were as they were than I was interested in playing games and sports. I partook of these activities of course, as they were mandatory. I did martial arts and played field hockey, but in my head, I was a philosopher.

I realize now that this is the luxury of being born into a middle-class family. The focus and guiding principle was always to follow what I wanted to do. I think many of us can relate that a young person lacking experience has no clue what they really want.

There are 2 Universal Truths I feel young people should know:

① *The Law of Diminishing Intent:* The longer we take to act on information the less likely we are to act at all.

② *The Paradox of Choice:* The more choices we have the less likely we are to make a decision at all, let alone the right choice (whatever that is).

Decision making is the most important skill we can learn. *And it is a skill!*

Most of us make Conditional choices.

For example:

- If it's not raining, I'll go for that run.
- If I can afford it, I will go to that event.
- If I pass the exam, I will decide what to do next.

Success in life depends on our ability to make Unconditional choices.

For example:

- Regardless of any circumstances, obstacles, or unforeseen eventuality I will succeed in my endeavor.
- My goal will never move and I will move forward until it is achieved.
- I will not allow my dreams to be compromised.

My choices in life took me to the ends of the earth and back again. I witnessed culture after culture on an endless quest to understand what unites all of us. I wanted to know how did I fit into this grand story we are all a part of?

Along my journey I picked up a working knowledge of transcendental meditation, Daishin Nichiren Buddhism, an honors degree in Anthropology, and learned a fair number of languages.

A wise man once told me, *"Observe what the masses do and then do the opposite."*

And so I did just that.

While traveling, a world recession hit, and I was thrown back into the "real world." I could no longer survive in my pursuits without a working economy around me. I fell into a sales position, selling door to door for commission only. Did I know anybody could get that job regardless of expertise or experience? Yes, of course I did, but I decided not to let circumstances influence my decisions.

This was the first time I had made an unconditional decision and it felt good.

I decided that day to make unconditional decisions from that day forward.

In most cases I succeeded.

Very quickly it became apparent that I had the grit and determination to succeed. Going door to door and hearing nearly one hundred NOs a day taught me to cut back on the non-essentials of my personality. I developed a thick skin which was needed to protect my core from becoming overwhelmed. Within 9 months I was running my own office with 18 people on my team.

For the next four years, I was immersed in the business of inspiring confidence in our sales teams, building leadership, teaching public speaking and motivational speaking every morning and every evening.

Success

We planned out territories, set up business trips to work different cities, launched one of Ireland's biggest energy providers, registered homeowners in the north of England for cavity wall and loft insulation grants, ran events selling cosmetics, and signed up hundreds of thousands of people to support a number of different globally known charities.

The one touch point that became apparent during it all is I saw how we are all spiritual beings. We are in a physical body having an emotional experience.

There is no escaping it.

It is this guiding principle that led me to an event in the Academy Plaza hotel on June 6th, 2015 where I was introduced to the *Thinking Into Results* process designed by Bob Proctor and Sandy Gallagher of the Proctor Gallagher Institute. As I sat in that room and digested the information being presented, I made another unconditional decision.

I was going to get my life on track and become the person I was destined to be. I would put all the potential to work that I was told I had from any person in authority I had ever met.

The days of half measures were over.

At that time professionally I was an International Inside Sales Manager for one of the world's top market research aggregators and I wanted more from life.

This material catapulted my financial results and set me on a path to freedom.

I realized the 'Genie' was me.

Chapter 2: What Is Holding You Back

"It's not who you think you are that holds you back, it's who you think you are not."

—Denis Waitley

Jackie and Lloyd separately traveled on different journeys to uncover what was holding them back from realizing their ultimate potentials. Why hadn't they fulfilled their destinies? What was holding them back?

In 2006, Lloyd sat on a beach in Thailand and received a text from a friend in Ireland asking, 'When are you coming back to the real world'? He wondered why would anyone want to live in the so-called real world when there were so many places on the planet that were infinitely more beautiful, and infinitely more simple?

"This is a feeling I held with me over the years and has informed my choices and my thinking from that day to this," Lloyd says. "What is it that leads us to believe that everything must be a struggle for it to be considered real? What if life can be effortless? What if everything you have ever wanted is just waiting for you to step out and take it?"

It is our conditioning and our paradigms that hold us back.

Lloyd believes that a beautiful, fulfilled life is your birthright and you have a responsibility to live your life to its fullest. But if changing your life, achieving your goals, making boatloads of money, traveling the world, and living in perfect harmony was so easy, wouldn't everyone do it?

Some do it, so the question was what did they know that Lloyd didn't? What stood between Lloyd and these others? "I realized that the next step of my journey was to figure out what had been holding me back from my goals. I was soon to learn I was in good company with many others who struggle with the same challenges."

The learning came quickly.

At the most basic level, what holds us back from meeting our goals is our struggle to fully believe, grasp, and accept our innate ability to succeed.

You might say you want it, but do you really? This can be quite tricky if the reasons for your ability to believe are on a subconscious level. Let's break that down even further, and look at the deep WHYs that stand in your way. Once you identify why so many struggle, you will learn how the art of "practicing what to do in real life" will lead you straight to success.

Let's address the several common key impediments to success that many of us have:

- Disbelief
- Discomfort with money
- Self-image
- Visualization
- Paradigms

Struggle with Disbelief

Disbelief starts inside as a reaction to others. We struggle with not believing we really can do it. Often, it's because we listen to what the world tells us about ourselves. We believe in the advice and opinion of others. We buy their stories instead of listening to our own. Despite feeling differently somewhere inside, we think they must know better; they must know what's good for us. We do what we are advised to do by a well-meaning friend or family member or we follow societal norms. This has created a society of the unfulfilled who often self-medicate with TV and 'noise' as we suffer in our search for some meaning in this world.

Jackie used to let life wash over her but, eventually, she decided to set off on a crusade of discovery. Early in her professional career she had a trainer who set a prime example of how, when you believe in yourself, success will follow. Jackie watched as her trainer built her business from the ground up. "She was a phenomenal success in her network business. She didn't listen to the naysayers. She went at it like a bullet and had complete faith in the business and the products. She believed wholeheartedly in herself, in her products and in her objectives. She had huge faith in the process, illustrating how the importance of belief and faith is necessary to succeed."

When Jackie started along the same path as her trainer, she was sure she had it down. While she experienced some success, she was continually frustrated with how everyone around her seemed to be flying faster and higher. "I was plagued with doubt and questions. I compared myself to others and constantly asked myself why I wasn't going as fast as they were? Was I too nervous? Did I believe enough in myself? Did I lack the discipline to do what needed to be done? I didn't want to bother all my friends and family with sales. What were they going to think of me?"

Jackie started feeling like a bit of a fraud. "I lived in a world of disbelief. I didn't believe. Not in myself. Not in the process." Jackie realized she lived in a world of doubt and was focusing on all the wrong things.

One thing that holds you back from succeeding is focusing on the things that are not positive and do not serve you. <u>If you have a disbelief in the positive, then you accept the negative</u>. Your paradigms or models are habitual behaviors that have almost exclusive control over your daily life. The majority of what you do is habitual. If you are not leading the life you want it is because <u>what you're doing is not in your</u>

own self-interest, and you are acting out of sheer habit. Yet we think these thoughts and take these actions and believe these beliefs anyway.

The question we need to ask ourselves is, why do we do that?

If you look at things such as what is serving you in life, you will see that your belief system plays a big part in it. Once you notice that your belief system or paradigm is not serving you, then it's time to rearrange it and that includes the way you look at yourself.

If you wouldn't put you forward for a job — why would anybody else?

If you wouldn't go out with you and have a relationship with you — why would anyone else?

If you wouldn't be a friend or a partner to you — why would anyone else?

Belief is at the core of many of our limitations. Lloyd experienced that it wasn't until he believed he could take control of his life that he was able to free himself from destructive behaviors. Your inability to visualize yourself succeeding is a key element of why you don't succeed. But happily there are proven methods to visualize that will allow you to take control of your future.

Struggle of Discomfort with Money

Low wealth consciousness is a terribly common problem. Yet this struggle is often hidden; secret and buried beneath many layers of self. You can believe you want money. You can visualize money. But are you truly comfortable with having it?

For many, the idea of having a lot of money is like landing a date with the best-looking guy or girl in town. You make plans for a date and you're already worrying. Is your car good enough? Do you have the right clothes? Will you have enough money for the night to be top notch? Are you good looking enough to be with him or her?

If you get through the pre-date worries you go to a party. Is your date looking at someone else who you think is more attractive than you? Was that a phone number he/she slipped somebody else when you were away for a moment? Why is everybody staring? Do they too think you're not good enough to be here with this date?

Given that mindset, what do you think your chances are that you'll even have a good time in the first place or land a second date? You wouldn't be any fun at all in that state! And most likely, you'll be more comfortable dating someone you don't feel is "out of your league."

Making big money is the same process.

We place a lot of importance on our ability to make money. To earn a good living where you can take care of yourself and your loved ones. If you're not feeling significant in your career, you won't feel significant as a human being. It's a downward spiral. Your self-worth suffers which affects everything else.

This is HUGE.

Even though we might think we feel differently, many of us are uncomfortable with having money.

Getting comfortable with money — making yourself at home with great amounts of wealth — is important so that once it truly arrives, you are able to welcome it with open arms. You feel it belongs with you!

Struggle of Self-Image

> *"Before you must do something, you must be it."*
> —Goethe (paraphrased)

Despite Lloyd's many successes, it became clear to him that it was his low sense of self-worth that ultimately slowed him down. "A carefree lifestyle had led to some destructive behavior around alcohol. I was always taking one step forward to take two steps back. This was a habit I had created over many years and it wasn't easy to break." Yet Lloyd knew he had to make a change in order to believe in himself. "I sat down at the front table at an event on June 6th, 2015, and all that changed. I made a decision to stop drinking alcohol for a year. I made this an unconditional decision and it completely changed my life, my relationships, and my sense of self. It allowed me to access my personal power and to work on creating a new paradigm for myself."

Lloyd always had a strong belief in his ability to understand things in life, but what he was lacking was the desire to act and the consistency to carry it out.

Just because you're outwardly confident doesn't mean that you don't also have self-limiting beliefs. Even if you have been conditioned by your upbringing and environment to be 100% confident in your abilities, and have had that experience reinforced by everyone you've ever interacted with, you may still have self-doubt.

There are people out there who are programmed to succeed in life and not doubt themselves, but it is very rare, and usually a result of an environment where the majority of their family and network are the same. It's called being 'unconsciously competent'. These people are not able to teach others how to do it as this is simply part of their subconscious programming.

The great news is that you can teach yourself to develop the mentality and the habits to succeed with intention. You can enjoy the same favorable results and have a strong self-image.

Considering your self-image sounds so easy, doesn't it? You merely ask, "How do I see myself?"

But the layers are deceptively deep. Just like in a video game, you only see the next level after you've broken through the previous one.

Most of us would never say to others the things we say privately to ourselves, would we? Would you tell a friend they look fat? Would you tell your child they will never succeed in life? Can you imagine telling your parents they don't deserve to have anything?

Self-image is a huge part of envisioning. Jackie used to let her poor self-image and self-doubt and others' doubt in her override her dreams. "I used to love to daydream, until my old *TIR*ed paradigms would snap me out of it and say, 'It's useless. Give up! Who do you think you are? If your mom couldn't make it, what hope do you have?'"

Jackie struggled with confidence. She struggled to believe she could make it. "You wouldn't believe the things I would think! I had some serious self-criticism going on. And when I wasn't succeeding, I was criticized by my family and friends. I was just starting to think and believe what everyone else was telling me. But this little voice whispered to me that I absolutely could be successful. I don't know why but deep, deep down I kept thinking, Hell, if those other guys can do it THEN I SURE CAN!"

The challenge is that these common struggles we face aren't solved tangentially, or one after another. Often, we're dealing with all of them all at once. Perhaps you can't visualize yourself sustaining the image. Perhaps you don't believe in it. Perhaps you're not comfortable with the money you'd make. If you can't see yourself doing it, if you can't picture it, then you can't have it.

It's that simple.

Simply wanting it is not enough, either. In order to visualize your way to a place, you have to have some level of belief. But that's not enough either. When your belief moves from mere wanting to a level of expectation, that's when the subconscious mind kicks in and starts to bring you what you want.

Imagine in your conscious mind that you have a belief. It's no more than a justification of a thought. This is not the same as faith. When you have faith, this is a belief that has been internalized and aligned with emotion. This is a principle-centered belief. When you have faith, it is not about convincing others or yourself that it is the right way to think but it is the guiding force in your journey and internal conversation. When you have faith, this becomes an emotionally deep-rooted paradigm; a habitual set of beliefs. At the core of who you are a mere belief is not the same as having faith.

When wants move from the level of wanting and belief that something is possible, to an expectation that it is going to happen — that's when you know your self-image has improved enough to be able to have faith.

To be able to do that in a practical fashion, you need to start looking at your sense of self-worth and self-love; how you think about yourself, how you talk to yourself. What is that internal conversation you're having? Which thoughts do you allow to have power in your mind?

We all have thoughts that come into our heads. Some don't make sense. Some aren't in line with our core value system. Some are not principally-centered thoughts but a lot of nonsense that's come in somehow. It arrives unfiltered in our minds from an outside source. And some of it is just plain garbage.

If you have a low self-image then you will allow external things to have an influence on your internal image.

This is where meditation comes into play. In meditation, you learn to grow your awareness.

Struggle with Visualization

Jackie heard that only 3% of people succeed in business. When she would ask how that was possible, she would be told that "they" must have something special in order to succeed. "Even though I didn't say it, I thought they had something alright — but if they could do it I could do it too! The question was how?"

This is a place where you become stuck despite the fact that you are loaded with potential. The paradigm takes what is logical to you and you allow it to make choices for you. Logic is an enormous big ceiling that you have been bouncing against all of your life. When you change the way you look at something — the thing itself will change.

Then there is no impossible.

There is no logic.

There is no ceiling.

These are all illusions.

The power, the juice, the money, the people, the connections... whatever is there to manifest this beautiful dream in your mind is right there with you.

Before GIAH you had to use your imagination. You had to visualize in your mind what a thing, a feeling, an event might look like. This isn't easy for everybody, and is downright impossible for some. With virtual reality you can create an alternative world and be able to see it with your eyes wide open. You don't have to try and imagine what it's going to be like because you can already see it.

This was the starting point for a concept that has grown wings and resulted in our *Visualization to Realization* course where we teach you exactly how to connect with your visualization and make it your reality. We're also creating a VR game which is in development right now and is going to change the face of personal development and visualization forever.

Jackie recalled sharing her C-type goal (dream) with her father's wife. "I said, 'I'm going to have a villa on the beach and my own house.' When I visited her again sometime later, I repeated the same thing and she replied, 'Yes, Jackie, you've been saying that for a while now. I've yet to see it come to fruition.'"

Immediately hurt and pissed off, Jackie was quite upset. "Who was she to say such a dream-crushing thing to me? My life wasn't over! I had plenty of time to meet my goals. I thought about her comment a few hours later and turned on myself. I felt more pissed off because I felt like a fraud or a dreamer when I'd been trying so hard to believe in myself. But I told myself that when working with C-type goals it's okay to be a dreamer because that's where the real magic takes place... in the imagination."

Your dreams are the starting point of creation. You draw energy from the universe, and through action it is expressed. In other words, the energy flows to and through you from your thoughts and into your reality.

Despite her work, Jackie struggled with disbelief and visualization. "I wanted success so much! I had worked on myself enough to develop the self-confidence necessary and I just knew I could be one of those 6–7 figure earners. I became frustrated with being told I was just not cut out for this work and I should pack it in. I started losing confidence in myself. I turned to food and wine for comfort because when I ate or drank I could temporarily forget. And that turned into a whole other bag of issues at home."

Jackie's husband knew her mother had died from cancer, and when Jackie mentioned that she felt her mother might have had a better chance if she had looked after her health a bit more, her husband turned the argument on Jackie. "He was worried about me. He was watching his beautiful wife destroy her looks and health. The once vibrant, fun, go-getter he had married was becoming a moody, dull, and lazy person. He had no idea how to motivate me. He said he was frustrated and didn't know what to do to get me to see sense and get back on track."

Jackie was angry with her husband for being so blatantly honest and sometimes cruelly so in an attempt to use the shock factor. Yet his words were having the opposite effect. "The more he came down on me and told me I needed to cop on, the more I despised him and his words. I would eat and drink even more to dull the increasing pain. Our relationship became so bad at one stage that I found it hard to be in the same space as him. Every conversation would go down a negative route. Spending time together became unbearable and I began to contemplate finding a way out. I could not visualize a happy marriage. The more I thought about leaving him, the more negative my thoughts became towards him. The more negative my thoughts grew, the more negative our relationship became. Something had to change!"

Friends of Jackie's had been through similar difficulties in their marriages and counseling seemed to work for them. "Counseling ended up being our saving grace. As soon as my husband decided he was going to make the effort to pitch up to one of our sessions, my mindset switched en*TIR*ely. I said to myself, if he is making an effort, he must care."

It was that switch in Jackie's mind and in her behavior that allowed her to visualize a different result. "The way I saw him began to shift. That's when we found our way again. Things started to change. Granted he was doing everything the counselor told him to do and so was I. In retrospect I am so glad we went through that tough period. We have been through so much worse in our years together. We had already weathered struggles in business, my custody battle, and poverty. It would have been a shame to allow our marriage to fizzle out after all of our other successes. If anyone tells you that marriage is an easy-peasy street of roses and chocolates I think they either got lucky or aren't being 100% honest. Like most things in life, success requires work!"

As a small child, Lloyd was very good at visualizing, and can easily recall how crystal clear his visions were. "I always had a brilliant imagination and I devoured books and fantasy fiction like it was going out of fashion. Yet somewhere along the way, I was drawn away from all that into a world of adventure and fun and the visions were forgotten."

An understanding of the deep inequalities around the world brought Lloyd to a point where he thought one person couldn't change the world. "I was familiar with the idea that you don't change the world by changing others, you do so by changing yourself, but I hadn't given it much credibility for a number of years. Studying with Ewa Pietrzak and following the teachings of Bob Proctor and Sandy Gallagher changed all of that for me."

Lloyd realized that everything he had and didn't have in life was a direct result of his own self-limiting beliefs, lack of faith in himself and in society in general. "This process changed my life. I'm now barely recognizable to myself compared to where I was. These changes came about due to having a coach and mentor through the process of learning to visualize effectively."

Struggle with Paradigms

Ultimately, we want to live a life of significance. Yet the paradigm is strong. Just like the world, it will kick you and hurt and drag you down to your knees if you let it. If you aim to go beyond what others think is possible, you will encounter resistance, and there is as much internally as there is externally.

When you grasp the power that the paradigm has over you, you will crash right through logic.

While Jackie was aware of the ground-breaking movie *The Secret* she didn't at first give it much credibility. "I was living in the world of 'hard work cures all ills' and 'willpower and determination are enough.' I found out that without belief, visualization, comfort with money, and a positive self-image, hard work is not enough. No good can come from doing the same thing over and over and expecting different results. Once I came into contact with the work of Bob Proctor, a new world opened up for me."

Jackie shares an example Bob Proctor uses to illustrate the power of the paradigm when it comes to belief and visualization:

> "It's mid-summer in Ontario and I'm sitting at my desk watching a small fly at the window fighting a losing battle. The fly is banging off the glass again and again in a futile attempt to smash through the glass. His destiny (or so it would appear) is to die right there on the window sill.
>
> If we were only to look at that area of the room it would seem like all is lost. If we draw back to the corner of the room and take a look at the scene we can see that barely 10 feet away is an open door, a sure exit, and freedom for the fly and more time on his journey but the fly can't see the window because it is focused completely on the struggle it is in.
>
> Now as far as we know the fly doesn't have an intellect so it is not to blame. It simply doesn't understand because it doesn't have the capacity.
>
> Also as humans we have an intellect and yet how many of us behave just like that fly in our own lives, in our own struggles. Because we lack perspective and don't scratch the surface or question the existing reality it becomes our prison."

Jackie found herself in that very mindset when it came to money for a long time. Then she discovered that not only do we all have a financial thermostat that stops us from any quantum leaps in our finances, but there is a way to break free.

Think back over the last 5 years and calculate what increase you have had in your wages each year. What is the percentage increase? Take your time with this and be honest. 5%? Maybe 10%?

Now take a moment to think of what figure would make your life comfortable. This will be a different figure with some higher and some lower but either way as you read you know exactly what it is.

Now, based on the percentage increase you have from the previous example, how long would it take for you to reach that figure? What age would you be? Do you expect to live to that age?

The internal growth Jackie experienced as a result of her earlier struggles showed her that what you think about, you bring about. This shift in mindset was to play a huge role in her future. "I saw that since I was thinking negative thoughts about business, having negative feelings about my marriage, and having negative thoughts about myself, the world only confirmed my negativity."

Naturally, Jackie wondered, given she had such envisioning power, what would happen when she shifted her mindset?

This comes back to the very beginning of visualization and visioneering, and belief.

Do I believe I can do it? Do I believe that I deserve to win? Do I believe that I have the necessary skills to win?

When you look back at your life in a historical context do you want your story to be a sob story or a tragedy or a success story?

Success does not always mean money. This is an important distinction to make. Among other areas, there is success in love and relationships, success in terms of personal fulfillment, and success in how we positively affected the people around us.

In this movie of yours, while you can be writer, producer, and director, you also have a part to play. *Are you a supporting actor, an extra, or are you the lead character? Are you the hero?*

So many of us play secondary roles in our own movie.

Society is set up based on the concept of competition. Small children are told they can do anything, be anything, and should follow their hearts. But very soon the rhetoric changes.

At the age of realization (around 6–7) children are told that they need to try harder, study more, brush up on certain things. This progresses until they move from primary school into secondary (or high school) and there is a huge shift. There are entrance exams and their future education is determined by a single exam and then children are segregated into a grade system. The quality of education will be determined by which grade they fall into.

Naturally, the 'best teachers' teach the 'best students.'

It is from this point that the modern education system permits these paradigms to take firm control.

When Lloyd was in high school he was told that artists are dreamers and very rarely amount to anything. "We know now that it is the people without a dream who rarely achieve anything of worth. We know now the schools were set up to educate workers so they can do their jobs better. They were not set up to help young people become the captains of industry. We were being taught to compete. We were not being taught to create."

When using visualization and visioneering you are working directly with the creative process. This all starts with goals, as life must have an objective.

It is essential that you make a plan. They say if you fail to plan, you plan to fail.

One of the biggest delusions of man is that there is any other cause other than his own state of consciousness.

Without belief there can be no future. Imagination alone will not get us there. It is from this point that your visioneering work shall begin.

Goals, Visions, Whys, and Purpose

Jackie had started the second round of *Thinking Into Results* when she got the idea to create *Genie in a Headset.* "I believe people can get very emotionally connected to their goal. Now you've got to get emotionally connected to your VISION, your WHY, and your PURPOSE. But NOT the how. For example, I felt I had to get into the *Voom* competition and I had to meet Richard Branson. It didn't happen at the time I planned. For whatever reason, the universe didn't plan it that way. I could have gotten really upset and made a decision that this envisioning stuff doesn't work which would have been understandable. What if I'd allowed my paradigm to say that it didn't happen; I didn't even get into the *Voom*, and what in the hell am I thinking? If I had done that we wouldn't be here today doing what we're doing."

> *"You can't connect the dots looking forward; you can only connect them looking backwards. So you have to trust that the dots will somehow connect in your future."*
>
> —Steve Jobs

"Only when you look back can you see how the dots are connected." This is where you trust that as long as you're connected to your VISION, your WHY, and your PURPOSE, it is going to be okay.

Sometimes you must wait and see without getting too emotionally involved if the plan isn't happening the way you thought it would. "We all have to remember that one of the laws we have to abide by is the Law of Gestation," Jackie says. "This law says that when an idea like a seed is planted in your mind and you are emotionally connected to that idea, then it has to come to fruition. It has to take place but we just don't know when. It can be a waiting game, but keeping that faith that it will happen is crucial."

Don't give up!

Jackie said there were many times when she wondered if she was actually going to make the Genie a reality. People asked her if she knew what she was doing? Did she have any experience in VR development? They told her not to be stupid. They said her idea was not going to work. They said it was like winning the Lotto. They said she wasn't business minded. "They said I didn't have the IQ level to make it," Jackie said. "There were quite a few people raining on my parade. What if I had decided that since I didn't meet my goal of winning the *Voom* competition and pitching to Richard Branson, that perhaps all those people were right?"

"When I approached an investor, he said my idea was too much of a 'pie in the sky' kind of thing. He said that it sounded too whimsical. He said no serious investor would take my idea seriously and besides, I didn't even have a business plan," Jackie said. "Let's just say that there were a lot of things coming up in terms of challenges, but I remained true to course as I was guided by intuition the en*TIR*e time."

While live-streaming Bob Proctor's *Paradigm Shift* course in Los Angeles, Jackie found herself watching the videos displayed while the attendees took breaks. The one video that stuck out for her was the advertisement for *The Matrixx*. "It was as if I was being guided; like someone was placing little golden bricks on my path to show me where to go. That was how it felt. The universe was giving me clues: do this, now do that, and now shift this paradigm or that paradigm." Jackie knew she had to get to *The Matrixx*. She didn't know why — she just knew she had to get herself there. "It was like magic to me. It felt like I was in this magical world of the

Genie and things started happening as if by magic. My intuition was guiding me and that pull to *The Matrixx* was so strong I just had to get there."

Everything shifted for Jackie at the event. When Bob walked down from the stage towards Jackie, she was talking to Sandy Gallagher and so she couldn't see Bob. As he got closer to her, he announced to the whole room that her idea was something worth investing in. Sandy Gallagher asked everybody in the room, "Who thinks that this is an awesome idea?" Jackie recalls that nearly everyone in the room raised their hands. These happenings solidified Jackie's feeling that she had a brilliant idea.

That sequence of events corroborated everything that Jackie had hoped and dreamed for. This eventual outcome was exactly what Jackie had visualized and she has used this same method to manifest so many great things since.

Jackie admits that her self-image wasn't quite ready to accept the reality at the time even though she wanted it so badly but, once it hit her subconscious everything she had been dreaming about, everything she had visualized was suddenly validated.

"When a person of Bob and Sandy's caliber is standing in front of you saying your idea is a really freaking cool idea, that's monumental. It meant everything for me that a person like Bob with so many years of experience would support my idea. Bob is not going to BS you. He's not going to tell you something is good if he doesn't think it's good. He doesn't do that," Jackie says. "It was so nice to hear it because at that stage I did believe that I absolutely wanted to make it happen."

After that, people changed their tune. Instead of hearing that her idea would never work, Jackie began to hear that she was going to be the next big thing. "I started laughing because I was thinking this is ridiculous! It was like I had moved into another playing field and it seemed completely surreal. That was me quantum-leaping through my very own paradigm shift!"

Within six days, Jackie had twelve investors wanting to invest in the business. She walked away with three investors and *Genie in a Headset* on its way. Within the space of a month the legal documentation had come together and GIAH International, the logo, and the branding were born. In the space of 6 months, Jackie began writing a book, a course, and developing the actual *Genie in a Headset* game. With Lloyds assistance, the course and book came into existence.

Chapter 3: They Made Me Do It, Those Nasty Gremlins

"When you really grasp the power that the paradigm has over you, you will crash right through logic."
—Bob Proctor

What exactly is a gremlin, you wonder? Surely we aren't talking about a Mogwai, or the small, destructive evil monster popularized in that movie *Gremlins* from the 1980s?

Or are we?

A gremlin is usually defined as "internal dialogue that veers toward the negative." If we were to tell you that the first gremlin we shall introduce you to is your own self-image, you are likely already acknowledging that small, destructive evil monster that lives inside your head. You probably won't be too far off.

Gremlin №1: Poor Self-Image

Your beliefs are shaped first by your self-image — that filter through which you view the world.

Ask yourself a couple of questions, and you'll soon see that you develop a self-image through your experiences in the world and then that's how you have been living your life:

- Do I have good, sound reasons for my beliefs?
- Where do my beliefs come from?
- How do I change my beliefs?
- Would changing my beliefs improve my life?

Self-image is generally going to be the biggest block standing in the way of our success.

"My mother is an editor and an absolute genius," Lloyd says, "but I can't remember ever getting a compliment not accompanied by a correction. For example, she would say, 'Great job, but next time you can try it this way.' The result is that I had this constant desire to be better; to always be better. While my mother meant her redirection in a nice way, it came off as not always pleasant in the sense that there was always a level of 'it's good but it ain't perfect — there's room for improvement.' I felt like I could have done more, and in many cases, I could have. That's where my self-image was, I may have achieved this and that but what have I really achieved? What right have I got to stand up there and tell my story?"

Self-image is a pervasive gremlin.

Am I good enough?

"I've done a lot of work on myself. And when I ask anybody else about me they say that absolutely I have a story to tell, but it doesn't feel that way to me all the time," Lloyd says. "It's only now I realize what I have achieved, and see that I'm actually doing what everyone else wanted to do but didn't do, because their fear held them back."

When you don't have what to you is a large amount of money in the bank, it can be difficult to accept that you're successful. But in the mornings when you see everyone else heading to their corporate jobs, and you're at home working on your dreams, you have to start looking at whether you are 'successful' or not. Working on your dreams is in itself a success because you've managed to figure out a way to do so.

There's a gestation period with anything. You start a new career or a new business, and it takes a period of time to lay the foundation and the groundwork. Laying the foundation for a business may require that you take a step back to take care of necessities while continuing to focus on building your dreams.

It doesn't always happen that way. Many people are too afraid to let go of the so-called security of a full-time corporate job. Lloyd says, "I was talking to someone recently whose job finished. She said that it was just so hard to find a good boss and meet their expectations. I told her that it's a bit easier when you are that boss. There's no time like the present for realizing that, because it's pretty obvious that there's no security in a full-time job. She was let go 3 weeks before Christmas!"

How does that feel?

Not very good.

Self-image is the biggest thing that stops a person from being successful.

Jackie says, "You have these people with absolutely brilliant minds, yet they lack self-worth: they don't believe in themselves. They listen to everybody else telling them why it cannot be done and they believe it; they don't end up being successful. You shouldn't listen to the people who say, 'You can't do this, you're not good at that, you're not suited for this kind of thing.' Who are they to say so? What made them the authority? I had immediately decided when my dad came home after being dismissed after 15 years with that company that I would have my own business.

"But I became a teenager and then a young adult, and I lost that drive," Jackie said. "I began to wonder to myself, 'Who do you think you are?' I never went to university, I didn't get a degree. I felt that a lot of people associate success in business and life with high intelligence and high academia. I didn't have that. I didn't concentrate in school as I should have. It's almost like some sort of report card syndrome where people see that you aren't very smart on the report card, so they think you must not have the wits about you to be successful in life. Since I didn't do well in school, therefore

I wasn't going to make it as a business person. My self-image was in the toilet."

Once Jackie began the *Thinking Into Results* course, she learned the importance of self-worth, and how to love herself again. "You learn to really respect yourself regardless of what other people say and what that 'report card' says. You can change those results. But the first thing that must change is believing in yourself: no one is going to do it for you. Just like that old saying, if you want someone to love you, you've got to love yourself first. If you don't love you, how do you expect others to love you?"

Jackie grew up feeling the lack, as many women do. "You don't feel like you're good enough or you don't feel like you have what it takes to be a successful business person. Women can feel like they can't do everything. They're taking care of the children and looking after the house and the husband and all the rest of it, there's a sense of 'I can't do everything. I might be good with the kids and the house, or I might follow some kind of career. Because I have to look after the children how could I possibly be a successful business person as well?'" It becomes almost overwhelming because there are layers upon layers of responsibilities.

In trying to find her "success," Jackie looked at so many YouTube videos and watched so many documentaries, and tried out so many things. "But without somebody to guide me through the process, I just felt lost."

As a man, the struggle manifests differently but with no less stress, Lloyd explains. "Men try to find a job that's a career because the expectation is that men must have a job/career because they're going to have to support a family. Women often have the option to do either. The perception is that women have three choices: they can have a job but not have a family, they can get someone else to work while they have the family, or they can work part-time and have a family. Men either have to work or they can't support the family. There is no option. This creates a tremendous amount of pressure for men."

When Lloyd turned 30 he realized he'd spent a lot of time doing what he wanted to do. "I traveled and I had all these amazing experiences. I did all the things everyone who went to work at a corporate office at the age of 18 didn't get to do. They were all miserable at the office while I was out having great fun." Then Lloyd realized he wanted to start having kids yet he didn't have a set career path that he'd followed. "I'd done all sort of different things but I had to ask myself now what the hell do I do? Where is this money to support a family going to come from?"

Of course Lloyd could have gone and built a career at a corporate office and followed that course but after having spent 10–15 years living freely, the thought of imprisoning himself in a cubicle and going home to a family he didn't get to see that often, because he was always at work, was not a very appealing long-term plan — for them or for me. "Ironically I got a job in a corporate office because that was where the money was and my goal was to build revenue to start a family."

But Lloyd was determined to find a way out of that system. "That was the driving force behind my starting *Thinking Into Results*: to find another way to live."

But Lloyd's poor self-image gremlins were strong. "I knew if I wanted to live in a way where I could share value, I must have some value, but I didn't know what value I had. I had a lot of experience doing different things and I knew a lot about a lot of things. I had a background in spirituality and meditation and lateral thinking and education and academia and acting and so on. So I knew I had things that were usable, I just had no idea what I could use them for."

Lloyd went into *TIR* looking for an idea. "One of the gremlins for me at the time was the realization that the way I'd been living my life until then was fine as long as I didn't plan on saving any money. I knew that if I wanted to have children and a family then my free-wheeling lifestyle was not going to be sustainable."

Gremlin №2: Lack of Faith

Shortly you shall meet the 7 Hermetic Laws, which are Universal Laws by which the en*TIR*e Universe is governed — three are immutable, eternal Laws and four are transcendable, mutable Laws. As stated in the Kybalion, "the Universe exists by virtue of these Laws, which form its framework and which hold it together."

For the time being, let's explore #5, The Law of Rhythm. Like a pendulum swinging side to side, rhythm compensates. You've seen this in your own life: all things increase and decrease, ebb and flow. Empires rise and fall, systems of law and commerce change and your vibration goes from positive to negative and back according to this Law.

To transcend this law, you must focus and exercise your higher faculties and employ faith in practice. You will know when the backward pendulum begins, and you will have faith to know it will return. Eventually, you will begin to swing higher and not be affected by the negative.

If you don't have faith, then during the down times you won't have faith that the pendulum will return and that the positive is coming back. With faith, you will know that it has to, as it follows the law of rhythm.

Life is cyclical by nature. If you don't have faith or any way of rooting yourself, you generally tend to think only from within the one experience you're having, and don't think outside of the box or take into consideration the bigger pictures.

The gremlins are a reflection of that internal conversation. For example, the difference between a pessimist and an optimist runs along the same lines. A pessimist thinks that circumstances are external and not controlled by the individual and can last forever. The optimist looks at the same set of circumstances and accepts that they're temporary and within their control.

The personal gremlins — those small destructive monsters — are related to our viewpoint according to our individual perspective. Oftentimes, the tendency is that if things don't work, we quit.

When first beginning her *TIR* work, the most important lesson for Jackie, more than anything else, was when she read Bob Proctor's book *You Were Born Rich*, specifically Chapter 4, "Let Go, Let God." "It's about having your goal written down, really believing in it and then letting it go into the universe. "You cast your goals and your dreams into the universe and then you let go and let God. It's really very much about faith: faith in yourself and the belief that you will ultimately hit your goal no matter what."

Gremlin №3: Belief in the Bigger Picture

People who accomplish great things are aware of the negative; however, they give all of their mental energy to the positive.

Before *TIR*, Jackie was struggling with her relationship. "I felt that there was no hope and that we were going to separate and that I just wanted out. Ewa kept saying to me, 'Stop!' but all I wanted to do was talk about my problems and how awful I was being treated as the victim. All I was doing was giving more and more energy to that, and it was just getting worse and worse and worse and worse. My husband said he could feel how much I despised him. He felt we were in big trouble as well."

Ewa's teaching was to be like the windscreen wipers. She advised Jackie to be very selective about what she allowed to affect her and keep an eye on the bigger picture. "It took a lot of practice but once I got it... I got it. I grew a stronger belief in myself. The more I believed in my goals and what I was doing, and the more I repeated the work in *TIR* — the more I solidified my goal and felt that I was worthy and that

I absolutely deserved success. I had a big paradigm around not being worthy of a lot of money. The paradigm spilled over into not being worthy of love because I still didn't have self-love which was a big thing."

Jackie had a great opportunity to beat her gremlins.

"I knew Richard Branson's *Voom* was happening where you put together a video and pitch a story. You get people to vote for you and if you are one of the top 10 who gets the most votes, you actually get the opportunity to pitch your business in front of this panel of judges. If you are the top 4 or 5, you then get an opportunity to pitch your business idea directly to Richard Branson himself. I knew I had to do this because VR is the new thing and everyone was going to want this. Lloyd and I were in the same mastermind group at the time. The *Voom* competition was only 2 weeks before it closed and other people had already had months in it to gather votes and so on," Jackie said.

"Lloyd offered to do the video for me, and when he asked when I wanted to do it, I said ASAP. I need to get this thing in before it closes. He was game, so we got the video together with 1 day of shooting and within the space of 3 days it was done and submitted to *Voom*. Next, I emailed everybody I knew to ask them to vote for me. Although there were loads of votes coming in, it was not nearly enough because I wasn't in the competition long enough. I only had 2 weeks and even though I even went on radio to talk about this I didn't get enough votes."

But that didn't matter.

"I was already on the journey to really believing that this could definitely be a viable business idea. Because we put the video together, I was getting amazing responses back from so many people," Jackie says.

The most amazing thing was that the idea went from the concept to what it is now by morphing and evolving into something so much bigger than what the original idea was.

"That happened because I attracted all of these talented people to make this happen. I got everybody I needed to get me to where I am right now. It was like the universe served them up on a plate directly to me. That's the only way I could describe the process.

The 333 story really resonated with Lloyd. "People don't think any bigger than their circumstances, and so they never achieve anything outside of what they can immediately see."

333 Story by Bob Proctor

Excerpt from Bob Proctor's You Were Born Rich

I was conducting a seminar, which ran from Thursday night to Sunday, at the Deerhurst Lodge, which is a resort approximately 100 miles north of Toronto. On the Friday night, a tornado swept through Barrie, Ontario, a town about 40 miles south of Deerhurst. The tornado killed a dozen people and did millions of dollars' worth of damage. On the Sunday night, as I was coming home, I stopped the car when I got to Barrie. I got out on the side of the highway and looked around. It was a mess. Everywhere I looked, there were smashed houses and cars turned upside down.

That same night, another gentleman, Bob Templeton, was driving down the same highway. He and I had never met, however, an idea from my seminar was about to bring us together in a lasting friendship. He stopped to look at the disaster, just as I had, only his thoughts were different than my own. Bob was the Vice-President of Telemedia Communications, a company which owns a string of radio stations in Ontario and Quebec. As he stood there viewing the disaster, he thought there must be something he could do for these people (with the radio stations he had). That thought kept returning to his mind that night and all the next day.

The following night, I was doing another seminar in Toronto. Bob Templeton and Bob Johnson, another vice-president from Telemedia, came in and stood at the back of the room. They were evaluating my seminar, trying to decide if I could help their company reach its goals, which I ultimately did. Because of Bob Templeton's influence, I subsequently worked for the en*TIR*e Canadian broadcasting industry. He loved what I was doing in my seminars because it was in harmony with his way of thinking. Bob Templeton became fascinated with the laws of the universe, particularly *The Law of Polarity* or as it is often referred to, *The Law of Opposites*.

This law clearly states everything has an opposite. You cannot have an up without a down, hot without cold or in without out. By the same token, if you can figure out why something you want to do cannot be done, by law you must be able to figure out how it can be done. People who accomplish great things are aware of the negative. However, they give all of their mental energy to the positive.

After the seminar, Bob Templeton went back to his office. He told me it was late but this one idea he picked up had him excited. It also had him committed to the idea of raising millions of dollars and giving it to the people who had been caught in the tornado, and he was going to raise the money immediately! Furthermore, he was not remotely interested in why he couldn't.

The following Friday he called all of his executives at Telemedia into his office. At the top of a flip chart in bold letters, he wrote three 3's. He said to his executives "How would you like to raise 3 million dollars, 3 days from now, in just 3 hours and give the money to the people in Barrie?" There was nothing but silence in the room.

Finally, someone said, "Templeton, you're crazy. There is absolutely no way we could raise 3 million dollars, in 3 hours, 3 days from now!"

Bob said, "Wait a minute. I didn't ask you if we could or even if we should. I just asked you if you would like to." Bob Templeton was wise; he was appealing to

VISUALISATION TO REALISATION

the charitable side of their nature. It was important for those present to openly admit that this was something they wanted to do. Bob Templeton knew that his new idea could show anyone how to accomplish anything they wanted by working with the law.

They all said, "Sure, we'd like to." He then drew a large T underneath the 333. On one side he wrote, 'Why We Can't.' On the other side he wrote, 'How We Can.' Under the words, 'Why We Can't,' Bob Templeton drew a large X. As he placed the X on the flip chart, he said, "Now there is no place to record the ideas we think of which explain why we can't raise 3 million dollars, in 3 hours, 3 days from now, regardless of how valid they might be."

He continued by explaining, "When anyone calls out an idea which suggests why we can't, everyone else must yell out as loud as they can, NEXT. That will be our command to go to the next idea. Ideas are like the cars on a train, one always follows the other. We will keep saying Next until a positive idea arrives."

Bob smiled and continued to explain that, "Opposite the X on the other side of the flipchart, directly under the words, 'How We Can,' I will write down every idea that we can come up with on how we can raise 3 million dollars, in 3 hours, 3 days from now."

He also suggested in a very serious tone of voice, that everyone will remain in the room until we figure it out. "We are not only going to think of how we can raise 3 million dollars immediately, after we originated the ideas we are going to execute them!" There was silence again.

Finally, someone said, "We could do a radio show across Canada."

Bob said, "That's a great idea," and wrote it down under, 'How We Can.'

Before he had it written on the right-hand side of the flipchart, someone said, "You can't do a radio show across Canada. We don't have radio stations across Canada!"

Since Telemedia only had stations in Ontario and Quebec, you must admit that was a pretty valid objection. However, someone in the back of the room, in a rather soft tone said, "Next."

Bob Templeton replied, "Doing a radio show is how we can. That idea stays."

But this truly did sound like a ridiculous idea, because radio stations are very competitive. They usually don't work together and to get them to do so would be virtually impossible according to the standard way of thinking.

All of a sudden someone suggested, "You could get Harvey Kirk and Lloyd Robertson, the biggest names in Canadian broadcasting, to anchor the show." These gentlemen are anchors of national stature in the Canadian television industry.

Someone clearly spoke out, saying, "They're not going to go on radio." But, at that point, the group yelled, "NEXT." Bob said that was when the energy shifted; everyone got involved and it was absolutely amazing how fast and furious the creative ideas began to flow.

That was on a Friday. The following Tuesday they had a radiothon, where 50 radio stations, from all across the country, agreed to work in harmony for such a good cause. They felt it didn't matter who got the credit, as long as the people in Barrie got the money. Harvey Kirk and Lloyd Robertson anchored the show and they succeeded in raising 3 million dollars, in 3 hours, within 3 business days!

You see, you can have whatever you want; all things are possible when you put your focus on how you can and "Next" every idea telling you why you can't.

This may be a difficult exercise in the beginning. However, when you persist in "Nexting" any and all negative concepts, the flow of positive ideas will roar into your marvelous mind.

Alfred Adler, the renowned psychologist, coined the extraordinary phrase, "I am grateful to the idea that has used me."

There can be no doubt that creative, forward-thinking ideas literally breathe new life into every fibre of your being. They awaken a part of you that you never even knew was sleeping.

Bob Templeton never received five cents for the leadership role he played, in marshaling 50 radio stations from right across Canada, to raise the three million dollars for the people of Barrie, Ontario in Canada. However, you must remember that this is truly an orderly universe; God's way of running this show is exact — when you put good out, it must come back.

I shared this story, when it happened, with two good friends of mine, Jack Canfield and Mark Victor Hansen. They were so intrigued by the story, they published it in their book *Chicken Soup for the Soul*.

A while back I was doing a satellite television broadcast for RE/MAX Real Estate with Mark Victor Hansen and he was telling me that, at last count, they had sold six million copies of their book. He also told me they are constantly receiving letters from people who read the '333 story' and use it to perform similar mental magic in their lives.

Think of it, millions upon millions of people are making positive things happen in their lives because Bob Templeton would not listen to the reasons why he and his staff could not raise 3 million dollars, in 3 hours, just 3 days after they began to brainstorm the idea.

By the way, Bob Templeton has told me he and his staff have formed the habit of '333ing' their wants and, as a result, he has gone on to become the president of Newcap Broadcasting company, a highly profitable corporation, with stations right across Canada.

It is my opinion that Bob Templeton has set up a force for good that will follow him wherever he goes. Profit has become his second name. Begin at once to '333' all of your wants and profit will follow you as well.

Gremlin №4: Following Through/ Staying the Course

Would Bob Templeton's story be memorable if he had stopped after raising the money, and sent the group home?

Of course not. He had to follow through.

Jackie once walked a difficult path of not following through. At first, after completing *Thinking Into Results*, she admittedly did not commit herself 100%. "I was a 'start it don't finish it' kind of person. I would start a lot of things and then I would not see them through to the end."

She felt angry when both her father and her husband pointed out this attribute of hers. "People put that into your brain and then you kind of live up to it. Anyway, I completed the course, and I was proud of that."

As we grow in ourselves we will always want to become better. Take Maslow's hierarchy of needs where he talks about getting to self-actualization which is the highest in the pyramid. Once your basic needs are met, then you are free to develop as you go higher and higher and higher. This is where people seek self-development and self-improvement.

"Look, there are going to be little paradigms but as long as it's not affecting you or your health in a negative way, it's okay to have little paradigms that you don't want to change," Jackie says. "But the ones that don't serve you, and there are probably quite a few, you need to tackle them. Tackle the strongest one first. Sometimes it depends on how ingrained that one particular habit is, to how long it takes you to crack that habit. And then you move on to the next one. Your whole life you're going to be improving and changing and changing different things."

"Bob teaches us the difference between reacting and responding to a certain conversation or the way people are towards us. Say you're in traffic and you sit on your hootah because you want to be frustrated. That's a paradigm. That's a habit. Because when you react, the situation is in control of you. When you respond, you are in control of the situation and you have a second between somebody saying something to you or somebody jutting out in a car or whatever the case is. You have that second to decide if you're going to react or respond? Not sitting on your hootah and getting all frustrated by somebody not driving correctly is just saying that that's just the way it is," Jackie says.

It's the same as when people get really riled about the economy, or a terrorist attack, or politicians, or the immigrants, or the refugees. So what? Unless it actually affects you and you can do something to change it, stop letting it control you. You have got to say, "It's time for me to take control and do what I can do about my life right now, right here."

> *"If one advances confidently in the direction of his dreams and endeavors to live the life which he has imagined, he will meet with a success unexpected in common hours."*
>
> —Henry David Thoreau

Belief Becoming Faith

There is a huge distinction between belief and faith. Believing something is true is no more than a way of justifying an idea, or justifying the paradigm (the gremlins).

True faith is expressed in action. When you have faith in something your fantasy goes from a mere want (believing it can be so) to an expectation that you will have it, regardless of external factors.

Faith is where our confidence comes from. When it comes to visualization, this practical faith is essential in order to maintain the vision of what you want on the screen of your mind. Daily reading and meditation practice are essential to this process.

Pablo Picasso said it best when he declared that *"everything you can imagine is real."*

It wasn't until Lloyd started changing his paradigms that he got a grasp of what kind of power they had over him. "I was brought up in a house without religion and so this idea of true faith was a little alien to me. Once I came to understand that my mind is a center of divine operation, everything started to shift. Your beliefs are inherited as your parents inherited them before you. It is not my place to say if one is true and another is false but I understand 'divine' to mean 'the part of me that creates'."

Understanding that we are all creative geniuses capable of much more than you might expect is fundamental to spiritual and personal growth. You are capable of exactly as much as you can imagine yourself doing.

When you step out and talk about your plans, people might say that you are foolish. They laughed at Edison but eventually he brought us the incandescent light bulb. They laughed at the Wright brothers, 2 bicycle mechanics whose father (a minister) told they them would go to hell for what they were doing and yet they introduced us to the world of flight.

This list goes on.

Story Time

Here is a short story to illustrate the importance of having faith:

> There was a business executive who was deep in debt and could see no way out. Creditors were closing in on him. Suppliers were demanding payment. He sat on the park bench, head in hands, wondering if anything could save his company from bankruptcy.
>
> Suddenly an old man appeared before him. "I can see that something is troubling you," he said.
>
> After listening to the executive's woes, the old man said, "I believe I can help you."

He asked the man for his name, wrote out a check, and pushed it into his hand saying, "Take this money. Meet me here exactly one year from today, and you can pay me back at that time." Then he turned and disappeared as quickly as he had come.

The business executive saw in his hand a check for $500,000, signed by John D. Rockefeller, then one of the richest men in the world!

"I can erase my money worries in an instant!" he realized. But instead, the executive decided to put the uncashed check in his safe. Just knowing it was there might give him the strength to work out a way to save his business, he thought.

With renewed optimism, he negotiated better deals and extended terms of payment. He closed several big sales. Within a few months, he was out of debt and making money once again.

Exactly one year later, he returned to the park with the uncashed check. At the agreed-upon time, the old man appeared. But just as the executive was about to hand back the check and share his success story, a nurse came running up and grabbed the old man.

"I'm so glad I caught him!" she cried. "I hope he hasn't been bothering you. He's always escaping from the rest home and telling people he's John D. Rockefeller."

And she led the old man away by the arm.

The astonished executive just stood there, stunned. All year long he'd been wheeling and dealing, buying and selling, convinced he had half a million dollars behind him.

Suddenly, he realized that it wasn't the money, real or imagined, that had turned his life around. It was his newfound self-confidence that gave him the power to achieve anything he went after.

Burning Desire

Napoleon Hill's famous book *Think and Grow Rich* made the world familiar with the phrase 'burning desire.' In June of 2015, Lloyd's burning desire was to be successful but he wasn't concerned with how he would make that happen. For the previous eight years, he had been constantly searching but wasn't really sure what it was he was searching for. "Thankfully I was invited to the seminar by my then partner, the wonderful Gosia. I can't even begin to tell you what a difference that single choice made to my life but I will give it a try."

Lloyd connected with Ewa Pietrzak immediately. He liked her energy. He liked what she had to say and he could tell she was a no-nonsense professional. "It was an 'aha moment' for me! This is just what I had been looking for... somebody to keep me accountable and put some shape on what I wanted, and more importantly where I should be coming from when I thought about my goals, and how I 'felt' about them."

All of Lloyd's successes up to that point had been achieved through grit and persistence and constant action. "Rarely had I sat back and attempted to connect with my vision on an emotional level. Nor did I give much thought to how I felt during the process. I was planning to be happy when I got there instead of feeling that happiness."

This is where Lloyd's story with the art of visualization truly began. "I discovered very early on that working hard for something we don't care about is called stress but working hard for something we love is called passion."

Lloyd knew it was time to engage his passion. "One thing I have always loved is the science of energy and how we as humans connect with that energy in our daily lives, how we communicate without words, how we love, how we understand and how we interact with the world around us. This was where my passion lay. So I knew I wanted to use the skills I had learned over many years motivating sales teams, teaching them to read body language, to paint pictures with words and from my acting to camera training, a start-up called *Change The Lens* was born."

Originally, *Change The Lens You Look Through* started as a simple concept. Lloyd wanted to help people — new business owners — tell their story to the world. As video converts better than any other medium Lloyd chose to do this through video. "I decided to make promotional videos for start-up companies in helping them create a narrative to pitch to camera based on their target audience and storytelling and some acting to camera techniques I learned while training as an actor as a younger man."

As it turned out and completely 'by chance,' Jackie mentioned on a mastermind call that she needed to make a movie to submit for the *Voom* awards. The top successful applicants would get a chance to pitch their concept to Sir Richard Branson, an accolade she was eager to secure for herself and GIAH.

Lloyd agreed to help. "I made a few phone calls, found a video editor through my personal network and we got to work. We had a week to make it happen. We rented a space in the Back Loft, just outside Dublin city's ancient city wall, owned and run by the enigmatic Miss Antonella. We were working against the clock. We were working against the changing light. We were working against the odds and yet thanks to the excellent editing skills of one Shane Conaty we were able to produce a beautiful narrative that put shape on an idea that up until then was simply a brainchild."

This is how an idea comes from something you hold in your head to something you hold in your hand. It is this video that formed the backbone of a pitch to investors, a narrative of the vision of what *GIAH* has set out to achieve and how it is placed to revolutionize the way that people visualize their goals and build personal development habits that reinforce that vision.

"On a personal note, the idea of *Genie in a Headset*, in my humble opinion, is absolute genius," Lloyd says. "The creative genius is a topic I have given a lot of attention to recently. Creative geniuses are heralded as different from humanity but in truth we are all creative geniuses. You won't find this taught at school, let alone universities. Mostly creative geniuses die broke and alone and are only recognized as such long after they are gone. It is not until we look back at their lives 'objectively' and see what impact they had in their genre, profession or industry that they are labeled as such."

Let's take that thought one step further. If you will be judged from the future as a whole, does it matter at what time in your life you created your magnum opus? Does it matter how one day in your life goes? Do you think that if you had an image of how you want to be remembered, that you would make a plan for that?

Imagine a movie with no storyboard, no director, and no producer. Do you think anyone would want to watch it?

The beauty of life is that it is *Life by DESIGN* and not *Life by Chance*. There are NO limitations except the ones we place on ourselves by submitting to the prevailing paradigms or conditioning we are surrounded by.

GIAH set out to change these paradigms in a fun way that enables and facilitates more growth and more vision while bridging the gap of work and play. "That's why I wanted to work with Jackie in creating *Visualisation to Realisation*, THE COURSE, and the book you are now reading," Lloyd says.

Motivation vs New Paradigm

Lloyd says, "People go to the event and decide they're going to make it happen. At an event you've got an emotional impact when you're there for a short period of time. It makes an impact on you. Motivational speaking has an impact on you for about 72 hours. It's important to realize that motivation and a new paradigm are not the same thing. It takes time to implement a new paradigm, and that comes after motivation. In *Thinking Into Results* we created habits over 6 months that serves for life as long as we continue to stay plugged in, and continue doing what we're supposed to do."

When you go to a workshop you can get really excited about something. "I wonder how many people go there with a fully-fledged idea and how many of them had people around them that were saying, 'Yes, you can!'" Not too many, I wouldn't think. As a society, we are hardwired for service and lack, and full of people who are more than happy to tell you why and how things can't be done.

One of the reasons why *Thinking Into Results* is so important, aside from the information, is the community that is built around it," Lloyd says. "It is very important to me that all of the people we mastermind with are the types of people who will tell you how things can be done. They're not the type of people that will ask me 25 questions about why I think it can be done."

Jackie says people tend to lose their motivation if their self-image is just not quite there yet. They haven't cracked that puzzle. Or they're not masterminding. Bob said it's so crucial to make sure that you join a mastermind group and surround yourself with people who are going to pick you up. "I was very lucky that I had people around me that I could come to when I was getting all that negative kind of bashing in the background. It wasn't that people were doing it maliciously. They likely thought what they were saying to me was for my benefit, like they were helping me. Where people's awareness levels are at is generally how they respond to certain things. So when they say negative things, they may not mean to be malicious. They may really believe they are helping you. But it's not in your best interest."

When you are surrounded by people who are like-minded, progressive thinkers and who are taking some kind of self-development course, wanting to improve, and grow their self-awareness — those are the people that you need to run toward. Bob's chapter, *Let Go and Let God,* really helped me with this. Being able to let go and believe everything will come to fruition in its own time has saved me so many times. I listened to that chapter when I was feeling like this was not going to happen or I was ridiculously stupid. What an absolute godsend that chapter was for me," Jackie says.

Chapter 4: I Am So Grateful I Know Those Laws

> *"Man's chief delusion is his conviction that there are causes other than his own state of consciousness."*
> *—from The Power of Awareness by Neville Goddard*

We are going to go a little deeper so that you can have a working understanding of exactly how we changed our paradigms. We help students from all over the world take control of their lives, find their life's purpose, and manifest it into reality using the principles we will discuss.

At the root of your experiences in the objective appearance of things and the subjective center of things, is your consciousness.

First, you must take responsibility for this.

The next step is desire. In order for the process of change to begin, a desire must exist to make the necessary changes in consciousness to allow the outer world to reflect these changes.

A burning desire is the birth of all great things!

Neville Goddard says, "All that befalls a man — all that is done by him, all that comes from him — happens as a result of his state of consciousness."

Another one of our favorite quotes of his is, "Whatever the mind of man can conceive and feel as true, the subconscious can and must objectify. Your feelings create the pattern from which your world is fashioned, and a change of feeling is a change of pattern." —Neville Goddard, *Resurrection*.

Visualizing has been endorsed by many successful people we know today such as Jim Carrey, Oprah, Bob Proctor, Sandy Gallagher, Tony Robbins, and Conor McGregor, to name but a few. They have used this skill as an essential tool for turning their dreams into reality.

The Secret refers to the secondary law, the law of attraction, and the tool used to attract what your heart desires. The primary Law here is *The Law of Vibration*.

<u>*The frequency we vibrate on determines how successfully we visualize.*</u>

<u>You already know how to visualize.</u> You have been doing it since you were a child. The only thing is, you didn't know you were doing it and because you didn't know, you allowed the picture to be influenced by external factors.

Whatever you focus on and picture on the screen of your mind will appear in its physical form whether consciously or unconsciously.

In order to engage in the art of visualization you must first consider how you sit in this process and what has been arresting your forward progression. What obstacles have been in your way? What has been steering you off course?

You must start by understanding what power you have to create change. In fact, it's crucial.

Descartes said, "Cogito ergo sum" (I think, therefore I am).

Thinking is the start of the creative process. What are you feeding your mind? What thoughts are you engaging with? What is your level of belief about yourself and your own potential?

Gratitude can be very useful in appreciating what you have. It's also helpful in using the emotion or the feeling of the goal fulfilled to influence your actions to bring about what you think about. This is crucial.

> *"The fact is no man can succeed in any pursuit unless he has a creative imagination."*
> —Warren Hilton

How to Use Future Gratitude

There is a 3-step process:

❶ Paint a picture in your mind in exact detail as you want it to happen

❷ Focus on this picture first thing in the morning and last thing at night, getting those details as clear as day

❸ Connect emotionally with that reality using gratitude as if it has already happened

> *"Assume the feeling of your wish fulfilled and observe the route that your attention follows."*
> —Neville Goddard

Gratitude is the fuel that governs your ability to manifest. It is the juice to your passion and is what ties you emotionally to your VISION and your LIFE PURPOSE.

Giving gratitude and developing strong self-beliefs are the starting points of discovering your unique life purpose, the BIG why for all you desire to BE, DO and HAVE in this lifetime.

Gratitude, like the universal laws of this universe, is not confined to a timeline.

What this means is that it is not confined to feeling gratitude for what you have right now. You can also feel grateful for things that *have happened* in the future just as you can feel grateful for things that have happened in the past.

Let's examine this idea. Life is full of ups and downs and none of us have had a singular upwards trajectory. Most have had high and low points in personal lives and careers. So when you look back at past events and feel gratitude for how amazing it was and how proud and full of contentment and gratitude you felt — even if you're not in that situation any longer — you can still connect emotionally to it every time you remember.

You can do exactly the same thing with facts and situations in the future.

In our course, we teach the 'I Remember When' method which creates a much deeper connection to the emotion of your *Vision*.

Your Why, Your What, and Your How

Your Life's Purpose is your WHY.

It's who you are at your core. It serves as the navigator for the decisions you make and the actions you take, and therefore the results you achieve. Bob Proctor teaches that once people understand their purpose, they have a high degree of mental clarity and self-awareness that makes them unstoppable. The goals they set become an expression of their values, gifts, talents, and abilities.

Your Vision is your WHAT.

This is your description of your ideal life. This is your inspirational story that you will work on and continue to grow and make bigger and bolder and more colorful.

You will revisit this many times in your life, and each time, you grow the picture in your mind. Like a painter, you will bring every brushstroke and every detail to life.

Once you become emotionally connected, this picture will feel more and more like your birthright.

Your goals are your HOW.

When you envision your ideal life and you set goals, this is how you live your vision. Goals give you direction and order in your thoughts to enable you to decide which daily actions you need to take.

Goals are like stairs. You climb up, you reach one, then you reach for the next, lifting yourself to your Vision. When you work through your Vision, your ideal life as you imagine it to be, create a wish list of the things you want, and you will start to discover amazing and interesting things about yourself and your most sacred desires.

The importance of gratitude cannot be emphasized enough.

It is only when you feel grateful for what you have in your life right now that you can open yourself up to more. Gratitude is a very powerful way to enjoy every day and be able to give thanks for the amazing things to come.

An important skill to develop is to feel thankful for that which you have already received and what it is you most desire.

Gratitude can change the way you see people and the way you see your own circumstances. When you start changing your thought process or perception on certain things, people and situations, you change your vibration.

Once your vibration changes you start attracting what you need to get what you want to be, do, and have. This is where gratitude can lend itself to the law of attraction.

A Famous Parable Related to Gratitude:

> There was a young, poor farmer in Scotland named Fleming. One day, while doing some work to get some money in order to feed his family, he heard a cry for help coming from nearby. He dropped his tools and ran to the place where the cry came from. There he found a terrified boy, half-submerged in a black swamp, screaming and struggling to free himself. Farmer Fleming rescued him. Had he not been saved

by Fleming, the boy would have died a slow and terrifying death by drowning in that swamp.

The next day a stylish carriage driven by handsome horses stopped in the poor farmer's front yard. It was very unusual to see such a beautiful carriage in those humble surroundings.

An elegantly dressed nobleman stepped out and introduced himself as the father of the boy Farmer Fleming had saved. He expressed his gratitude and said, "I want to repay you. You saved my son's life."

The Scottish farmer was amazed. "No, I can't accept payment for what I did," he said, waving off the offer. At that moment, the farmer's own son came outside.

"Is that your son?" the nobleman asked.

"Yes," the farmer replied proudly.

At that moment the nobleman got an idea and said, "I'll make you a deal. Let me take him and give him a good education. If this boy is anything like his father, he'll grow to become a man you can be proud of."

And so it was agreed.

Farmer Fleming's son graduated from St. Mary's Hospital Medical School in London and went on to become known throughout the world as the noted Sir Alexander Fleming, the discoverer of Penicillin.

Years afterward, the nobleman's son was stricken with pneumonia.

And what saved him?

Penicillin.

The name of the nobleman?

Lord Randolph Churchill.

His son's name?

Sir Winston Churchill.

What You Want Wants You

Know that everything you have ever wanted is waiting for you to come and collect it. If you employ your faith in your desire just as you would a fact in the past which is also nonphysical, you can and will manifest it in your own concrete reality.

Manifesting means experiencing the results of these concepts in your world. You are visualizing right now and you always have been. You have not yet learned how to keep the picture of what you want on the screen of your mind with focus for long enough to manifest it in concrete form. Your image is always changing because you have not learned how to keep it still.

We teach how to exercise your WILL, another of your higher faculties, to get your vision clear and just watch the results! We are working with the LAWS here!

The 7 Hermetic Laws of Ancient Kemet

"The Principles of the Truth are Seven; he who knows these, understandingly, possesses the Magic Key before whose touch all the Doors of the Temple fly open."

—from The Kybalion

As mentioned earlier there are 7 major Universal Laws by which the en*TIR*e Universe is governed — three are immutable, eternal Laws and four are transcendable, mutable Laws.

"The Universe exists by virtue of these Laws, which form its framework and which hold it together."

Knowing these Universal Laws and the basic Law of Attraction, and learning how to transcend the mutable Laws, is fundamental to changing the circumstances of your life so that you can consciously create your intended reality and achieve true mastery.

The first three laws are immutable, meaning they can't be overcome or altered.

1. The Law of Mentalism

Everything has its source in Mind. Everything we can see and experience has its roots in the invisible mental realm. There is a single Universal Consciousness known as the Universal Mind from which all things manifest. Our Individual Mind is an extension of the Universal Mind so also has the ability to create physically from mental energy. This is true mind power.

2. The Law of Correspondence

The concept was first laid out in the *Emerald Tablet* (or *Tabula Smaragdina*) of Hermes Trismegistus: "That which is Below corresponds to that which is Above, and that which is Above, corresponds to that which is Below, to accomplish the miracles of the One Thing."

What this means is that there is harmony, agreement, and correspondence between physical, mental, and spiritual realms. From the smallest electron to the largest star, All is One. There is no separation between anything in this universe.

3. The Law of Vibration

This Law tells us that nothing rests, everything moves, and everything vibrates. Science has also confirmed that everything in the universe is pure energy vibrating at different frequencies. Secondary to this is the Law of Vibration popularized by *The Secret*, which is a secondary law. Your thoughts are vibrations and "like energy attracts like energy," so we know that you get what you think about. Unconditional love is the highest emotional vibration, while hate is the densest and most base. We are learning to control our mental and emotional vibrations here. This is true thought power.

4. The Law of Polarity

This tells us that everything is made of a pair of opposites. It is the first of the mutable laws or transcendable Universal laws. Things that appear as opposites are only extremes of the same thing. The same applies to love and hate, peace and war, positive and negative, good and evil, yes and no, and energy and matter. You can change any of these with a simple raise in vibration.

5. The Law of Rhythm

Like a pendulum swinging side to side, rhythm compensates. All things rise and fall, ebb and flow. Empires rise and fall, systems of law and commerce change, and your vibration goes from positive to negative and back, according to this Law. To transcend this law, you must focus and exercise your higher faculties and employ faith in practice and you will know when the backward pendulum begins, you will know it will return and eventually you will begin to swing higher and won't swing as far to the negative anymore.

6. The Law of Cause and Effect

The is known as Karma. Every action has an equal and opposite reaction, every cause has its effect and every effect has its cause. The inner is the cause and the external is the effect. This is the essence of thought power. Every one of your thoughts and actions sets in motion a special effect which will materialize over time. To become the master of your destiny you must master your mind and accept that it is the cause of everything in your universe. In the process of creative visualization, cause and effect on the spiritual plane happen instantaneously, but on the physical plane we have the concepts of time and space, so our cause and effects seem to be separated. It is necessary to employ perseverance, practice and continued concentrated energy to manifest it in a shorter time frame.

7. The Law of Gender

This is the masculine and feminine principle of Yin and Yang. Everyone has the inward and outward expressions of feminine and masculine qualities. Love, patience, intuition and gentleness and energy, self-reliance, logic, and intellect.

They exist in latent form in all of us. We just need to tap into them. So, we are all complete, and so we say, you are pure, perfect, and complete.

Once you understand these Laws and learn to work with them instead of against them, a whole world of opportunity and achievement will open up for you.

Chapter 5: Higher What?

"When you change the way you look at something, the thing changes."
—Wayne Dyer

We have six higher faculties: imagination, intuition, will, perception, memory, and reason. They are hugely misunderstood, as well as underutilized! We're here to change that.

For example, there is a common misconception that you can have a bad memory or a good imagination, but neither is actually the case. Your higher faculties are like a muscle. If they are exercised they will be strong, if they are unused or inconsistently set to work they will become weak.

In our course, there are exercises you can do to improve each and every one of your higher faculties. Just like the Laws of the Universe, once you understand them you can set them to work for yourself.

How to Train Your Higher Faculties

- Imagination: Freeflow/Visualization
- Intuition: Listening/Feeling
- Will: Focus/Unconditional Decision-Making/Meditation
- Perception: Educate Yourself/ Reading/Re-Framing
- Memory: Memory Games/Gratitude
- Reason: Problem Solving/Listening

Each of these trainings is covered in detail in our courses, but here are a few suggestions in the meantime.

Mind Work

Lloyd describes himself as a very action-oriented person. "I used to work on will, determination, and grit only, but this hard approach creates a vibration that is at odds with the end goal of deep satisfaction and calm. For this reason alone, mind work is so important."

So what is Mind work?

Meditation

Of course, meditation is one of the more well-known types of mind work. There are many different types of meditation. You can pick any type that resonates with you but ultimately the goal with meditation is to learn how to be at ease with your own mind and to be the one who is directing the thoughts and how they are processed.

This sense of personal power is so important especially in this time of social media, smartphones, and the constant state of distraction we are subjected to.

The easiest place to start is with guided meditation which is very powerful. Lloyd says, "I like to use Deepak Chopra — *Soul of Healing Meditation*. I find this particular meditation to be particularly empowering. There is so much more to this life and our innate abilities to both control and to heal ourselves and it is amazing to feel this power firsthand."

Imagine you are going out on a survival expedition. You will be required to survive only on what can be found in nature. Do you think you would have a better chance of survival if you had a guide who had the knowledge of thousands of years of woodlore, so you only ate what was safe? Or do you think you would fare better tasting whatever you saw that looked edible, using a system of trial and error?

The phrase "standing on the shoulders of giants" comes to mind.

Guided meditations are very helpful for beginners in particular. For the purists, unguided meditation is great once you know the process. We have, in our course, a unique guided visualization meditation composed specifically for *Visualization to Realization* by the magnificent Hanne Deneire on the marimba at a frequency that speaks directly to the subconscious mind.

Visualization

We are the only creature (as far as we know) who can visualize and yet we allow other people's opinions and society's pre-conceptions to limit our imaginations. What is astonishing is that our imagination is limitless! Ask any parent and they will tell you amazing stories that their children come up with. The creative imagination is responsible for every single advance of man since the beginning of humanity. Yet for many of us, we can't imagine a perfect future or perfect reality for ourselves. This is the result of nothing more than conditioning, and it can be reversed!

Great news for all of us.

Daily Practice

If you are not already doing so, you should definitely develop a habit around doing meditation and visualization on a daily basis to exercise the higher faculties of will and imagination. It will help you so much!

In meditation, you use your will to remain in a calm state; being completely still and completely silent. With visualization you're willing a picture to stay in your mind, and to see the picture vividly, while using imagination to create a picture or story in your mind. That's true mind power.

Breathing

Breathing is used in almost all forms of meditation and visualization exercises to bring us to a calm state and lower our blood pressure and heart rate. This is the key to access the power of your body and mind.

Bob Proctor mentions "constant space repetition" and what he means by that is you have to do something repeatedly in order to get it. Even though it might seem illogical to do it over and over again, you do it anyway. For example, say you are completely solidifying negativity repeatedly in your brain. It's the same as telling someone you're sick even though you're not. If you say it enough times to yourself, you're actually going to start believing that you're sick. You can make yourself sick without even knowing it. THAT IS HOW POWERFUL YOU ARE! That is how powerful our minds are.

What sets us apart from any other living creature in the world are these higher faculties and the more we use (practice) these higher faculties, the more we become aligned vibrationally with our dreams/visions and our main focus in life. The more we understand it, the more we practice it. With concentration and focus, we move to where we need to be in order to attract the things we desire. We begin to shift those bad habits that don't serve us: weight habits or career habits or money habits.

Jackie clearly recalls the first time she felt she had at last visualized properly and realized she was emotionally connected to her visualization — a key component. "Previously I battled to visualize and I battled to see the picture clearly, to hold the pictures with my will. I thought if I'm battling to do this, there's got to be plenty of other people out there who struggle to visualize and hold those visions too. If we could only have our visions in virtual reality that would just solve all these problems of trying to see our pictures vividly."

Jackie imagined people seeing their visions vividly; experiencing them in virtual reality. "This way it would be much easier to become emotionally connected because instead of trying to visualize with your eyes closed, you would actually be in your visions with your eyes wide open."

Proctor Gallagher's *The Matrixx* is a 6-day event where ideas are created, developed and monetized. At *The Matrixx*, Bob Proctor, Sandy Gallagher, and their team work exclusively on developing and bringing ideas to life through a dynamic, proven and powerful process. Jackie wanted to join in on the benefit of sharing resources in an organized networking exercise with 100–200 like-minded attendees. Once she heard about *The Matrixx*, she knew she had to go.

"I didn't know how I was going to get there, so I used visualization. *The Matrixx* is a high-ticket event that ran $15,500 at the time," Jackie said. "I had done *Thinking Into Results* twice by then. I had done the Streaming Club. On the *Paradigm Shift*, there was this video about *The Matrixx* and I think they had a couple of other events on as well, but it immediately grabbed me. It was all about business and business ideas and building multiple streams of income and networking." Jackie knew if the Genie was to be born she had to get herself to *The Matrixx*. "The pull was so strong that I knew that it was the universe guiding me in that direction. I knew that I had to go! I asked Ewa what she thought, and she said, 'You'll find your investors there.'

"Oddly enough, now she can't remember saying that to me. She said it must have been her subconscious talking," Jackie explained. "Yet to me, it was the one thing that stuck in my head. I knew I had to make it happen because I would find my investors there. Since Ewa had been to *The Matrixx*, I figured she had to know something."

Jackie immediately began a visualization process. "I started visualizing myself in the plane. I imagined looking out the window of the plane, down at the clouds, and feeling that excitement of, 'I'm on my way to Toronto now!' I'm not a great flyer, so when the turbulence hits the airplane I get this funny feeling in my stomach, a nervous kind of feeling."

Jackie knew she had finally succeeded in visualizing when she actually felt that nervous feeling as if she was already on the plane. She said to herself, "Whoa, okay now I'm getting it, now I get what visualization is all about!"

With young children at home and only a business idea in the bank, Jackie set about finding the money to attend *The Matrixx*. Two weeks after that visualization experience she had booked her ticket from Ireland to Toronto. "It happened very quickly. I was going around to the banks and asking them for loans only to be told no because I didn't have any credit history. Now how was I supposed to get a credit history if the banks wouldn't give me credit? Didn't make sense, but I didn't let that stop me. I went around to 4 or 5 different banks and I was told no each time. Next, I got a credit card with a thousand Euro credit limit," Jackie says. She was still $14,500 short, but she took a leap of faith and put the thousand Euro down on *The Matrixx* as a deposit to signify that she was absolutely going.

Jackie didn't know how she was going to get the rest of the money. She just knew it was going to manifest from somewhere. "That's what you call true faith," Jackie laughs. "And, let me tell you something: I got the money from an unexpected source."

Next Jackie was faced with another decision. The money she received was enough to build a small prototype of the Genie, and Jackie had to decide whether to take a chance and put the money down to pay for the event, or to build the prototype to get investors. "The pull kept saying to go to *The Matrixx*, but I wondered if it would be better to build the prototype instead?"

Jackie called around to trusted friends to help with her decision. When no one picked up the phone, she initiated the wire transfer to Proctor Gallagher Institute and boom — the money left her account. "I hit my terror barrier. I wanted to throw up. My gremlins started coming up and piling onto each other and I wondered, 'Have I done the right thing here?' My phone rang and it was Monica, and she said, "We've received your money. Congratulations! You're going to *The Matrixx!*"

A sudden peace came over Jackie and she knew she had done the right thing. "Then I got really excited because I knew that everything was going to be okay. It just shows that visualization is incredibly powerful. Once I had that experience, it happened so quickly. *The Matrixx* happened, and the investors happened, and now I have so much faith in what I'm doing."

Jackie truly believes in every single thing she is now teaching other people. She witnesses how quickly she is able to manifest now. She laughs, "I am a Genie now! What I think about all the time happens rather quickly. I am a total 100% believer in what I've learned and what I now teach. I attribute it to the fact that my faith is so strong that it's now easy for me to manifest things the way I do."

She is sure to remain vigilant about the quality of her thoughts. "If I think something I don't care for, I have to very quickly say, 'Cancel it! Cancel it!' I believe because we have been working so closely with this material as we put together this course, and we're working with people and instilling high-vibe information on such a high level, we are teaching people to raise their vibration. Simultaneously, we're raising our own levels of awareness. It's not about teaching someone something because you can teach anyone anything. With this type of material, you have to walk the talk. Because you're practicing what you're preaching and you're telling people to do the same, it starts happening very quickly for you.

"You're not just the student anymore. I saw what was happening with Ewa and how it was so easy for her to manifest people into her events, and how powerful her manifestation and visualization were because she was not only coaching but doing everything she was telling us to do." Jackie says. "It's pretty powerful stuff. If you want to be working on a particular goal, do the mirror work and the mind work. It is so powerful."

Once upon a time, Lloyd worked in a corporate office. "I had a sales role in digital marketing and in direct sales. At the time I was making around six grand a month in gross sales. Obviously, for a man with goals and dreams, that was nowhere near where I wanted to be. I didn't have the right habits because I didn't think I was suitable for a corporate environment. I'm the sort of person who likes to do what I want to do, not what other people want me to do."

Lloyd decided to use mind work to better his numbers. "I'm very focused on what I want, so in short time I was able to turn that around very quickly from doing mind work and mirror work (we will get into that later in the book) and increase my sales to 207,000 within six months. Previously it would have been 36,000 based on an average of 6,000 a month.

"That was fairly significant for me. While there were many others, this was one of two major things that I got from doing these mirror and mind work exercises," Lloyd continues. "One of which was a part of *Thinking Into Results*, the lesson on self-image. There's a part where it asks you about being the star of your own movie. There's a particular part where you think of what house you want to live in, and I thought, 'I want to live in a four-bedroom, detached house on a quarter of an acre with trees all around the outside, completely enclosed with a big gate.' I went to the mirror and repeated this six times, 3 times into each eye (more on that later). I told myself again and again in the mirror that I was so happy and grateful now that I live in a four-bedroom, detached house."

About three months later somebody asked Lloyd, "Hey do you remember that exercise in *Thinking Into Results* where you talked about the house you wanted to live in?" When Lloyd replied that he did remember, the friend asked, "Which house did you want to live in?"

Lloyd said, "A four-bedroom detached house on a quarter of an acre."

"Isn't that where you live right now?"

It was true. "I'd moved into a five-bedroom detached house on a quarter of an acre with massive trees all around it, and with electric gates. I didn't even notice that it had anything to do with the fact that I said it to myself in the mirror. I said it for what must have been five weeks three times in the left eye, three times in the right eye every morning. I forgot about it because I moved on to the next lesson in the program and had other tasks to do."

Take a Step Back

Caught up in the flurry of creating the Genie, Jackie didn't stop to think about the journey until a friend urged, "Jackie, take a step back and look at what you've done."

Jackie didn't understand what she meant at the time. "I wanted this so badly, like just so badly. There's a saying 'If you want something so badly you can taste it.' That's how I feel; so I live, eat, breathe, and sleep GIAH. This is who I am."

Sometimes you don't realize when you're in the thick of a thing just how much you've accomplished until you look back and connect the dots, as Steve Jobs said.

"I understand that people from *The Matrixx* tend to give up if they haven't kept in touch with the other people. They haven't been masterminding with the right people. So they lose it because they live outside and they let that feeling of 'I am so amazing! I can accomplish anything!' slip away once they leave *The Matrixx*. You're on a high for 2–3 months but then life can get in the way. It takes a hell of a lot of will to stay focused," Jackie says. "This is where higher faculties take center stage because you really are exercising them to still keep that dream alive."

Masterminding

One of the things that hold people back, apart from poor self-image (and obviously self-image is hugely influenced by mirror work and mind work and affirmations and things like that), is other people. Masterminding is key because other people who are not in the mindset of possibility becoming reality, and positive thinking influencing the external world, are living a world where they think external factors are not within their control. They believe they are constant, and never going to change.

Lloyd explains how three hundred years ago Isaac Newton and Charles Darwin changed the world's paradigm to answer the questions, 'Who am I, and where do I fit in the universe?' "They moved the answer from being explained only by biblical references and theological explanations to a hard science explanation. People started to think in a different way from before."

Darwin said that everything was based on conflict and competition. He looked at carnivores in nature and recognized that competition was there, of a sexual kind, so they could pass on their DNA. He extrapolated that out to include humans. Since then we realized nature works on a principle of cooperation and mutual aid.

If we look under the forest floor, for example, mycelium connects and transfers nutrients from one tree to another. If one tree in the forest does not have enough nutrients or is dying, the other trees will give it the nutrients that it needs to survive because they recognized that all of them must survive for any of them to survive. That's the model of nature that humans are now starting to recognize.

Lloyd says, "If you take away religion and borders and countries, we really are all part of one human family and we all have a very similar experience outside when you take away the bullshit. We're all just trying to express ourselves and learn where we fit in."

When you become aware it doesn't necessarily mean that people around you are becoming aware. You wake up and recognize that people are still half-asleep. When you tell them I'm going to do this, or I'm going to do that, they think that you're out of balance; balance meaning you're an average individual who does average things.

When you're trying to do extraordinary things, you're not in balance. (according to the rest of the people) You're out of balance because you need to be if you're going to expect to have different results from other people. For many reasons, (generally because they care about you and think they're doing you a favor), people tell you why the things you propose can't be done. They seek to bring you back into balance with them and their paradigm.

Because you have been a certain way for a number of years and have certain boundaries and it's expected those boundaries will stay the same. Everybody knows where they stand. But when you change, you surprise those around you.

It's like this. You think you know somebody, especially if you're in a relationship. They know you. This is who you are to them. And when you start to change and become somebody new, they become confused and wonder where their part is in your transformation.

When we started *Thinking Into Results* together all of the participants were waking up at the same time. They were all moving towards understanding a world where we talk about the way that things can be done, not about why things cannot be done. All of the gremlins that come up — whether they're self-image stuff about you, how you feel about your potential, whether you carry negative self-image from what people have told you in the past, whether you've suffered verbal, physical, mental or any type of abuse, people telling you that you can't do things — these must be addressed.

That's why masterminding is crucial. Without masterminding with like-minded individuals, it's going to be very hard to walk upstream when everyone else is coming downstream.

Even fish have figured this out. The salmon swim upstream to spawn and they know they must come up together; they don't come up on their own. They travel as a group because some will be eaten, some will be bashed on the rocks. With better numbers, they have a better chance.

Because of masterminding there have been many businesses that have started from a collaboration between people from *Thinking Into Results*. People have developed multiple streams of income and done very well.

From time to time, a person comes along and expresses an interest in having another stream of income but they have no idea where to start. Someone will help them. There's no level of competition in a mastermind. Instead, it works with a spirit of cooperation.

Masterminding really opens you up. You meet people and learn new things about your community. When you mastermind it's all about helping each other and seeing how we can make each other successful. Here is what Napoleon Hill had to say about The Mastermind:

> "It is the principle through which you can accomplish in one year more than you could accomplish without it in a lifetime if you depended entirely on your own efforts for success."

There's a way that you can connect with universal intelligence, Lloyd explains. "All people past, present or future are connected to universal intelligence. Time and space don't exist in the nonphysical world anyway.

You can, in fact, connect solely in your mind with a mastermind; they don't have to even be alive, you don't have to know them, you don't have to have ever met them, and yet you can actually mastermind with people because you're connected to all information at all times."

One of the things Lloyd always wanted to do was to create a mastermind outside of *Thinking Into Results*. "I never quite managed to find people of the right mindset to be able to do it YET. Now obviously that's the principle of *The Matrixx*. Each person goes to *The Matrixx* with an idea or maybe just the feeling of an idea knowing that someone there can help make it happen. This is exactly how Jackie put her idea for the Genie out there."

Jackie explains there is a snap session in *The Matrixx*. "You get a couple of days learning in-depth information from what Bob and Sandy teach you, and they get into your fantasy goals and help you come to know your purpose and what you are working toward. They cover different topics over the first 2 or 3 days and then they hone into multiple streams of income and business ideas and making a million look small."

How it is you can make a million? But break that million down so it doesn't seem like it's a big amount. It becomes really small and so believable, that you see anyone can make a million if you break it down.

Next participants work on their goal statements. "Once you've done this, you spend about 48 hours honing your goal statement. You can do questions and answers with Bob and Sandy, while Peggy walks around to help with goal statements. There's a lot of chewing and throwing, so they concentrate heavily on this," Jackie says.

One of the days they do the snap session in a big ballroom type of conference room, which is set up with tables in a circle. All the tables have 8 to 10 people each. You are given 90 seconds at each table in which to pitch your idea to these people from your goal card. You have this little goodie bag. It's almost like your bag of trick or treats because everybody has a card with their details on the back of it and on the other side is how they can help you.

"The first step is to approach each table and say, 'I'm so happy and grateful now that my business is XYZ.' You thank them in advance for helping you, then you say, 'What I'm looking for is X, Y, and Z.' There's no talking with them. They just write down on the card what they feel they can help you with, and they pop the card into your bag and then the music stops and you move on to the next table. It's almost like a speed dating session for business. You pitch your idea, and then you go from table to table and then you go all the way around until you're back in your chair," Jackie says.

By the end of the session, each attendee has a bag full of the contact details of people they can seek help from. "Everybody broke for lunch and we were told when we came back we were going to do some kind of closing afterward. Everybody else went to have lunch, but I ran up to my hotel room and threw all the cards onto my bed and sifted through them all to see who was interested in investing."

Because that was the last day of *The Matrixx*, Jackie told herself that by the end of this day, she would be face to face with investors. "I thought if I let it go without making contact, that life would get in the way. From the cards strewn across my bed, I saw that I had 12 people expressing interest in investing in my business. I knew I had to find those 12 people, because what if they couldn't remember me from the other 100 who were at the event? I gathered all the cards together and went searching for them. I found 8 of the 12 and out of those 8, 3 ended up investing which I felt were the best ones to move the business forward. If you use *The Matrixx* cleverly and you're very focused on your intentions, you'll get results. I got 4 times the amount of money back that I invested in getting there. It was the best decision I ever made," Jackie said.

If Jackie had taken that money and put it in a small prototype as she'd considered, she wouldn't have been able to build what she is building now. "Because of the investors and because of also looking at multiple streams of income, I learned to stretch my mind. I looked within my company to figure out how I can create multiple streams of income: the book, the courses, the game, and other things. I can't recommend *The Matrixx* highly enough because it literally shifts you to 5 levels into the stratosphere," Jackie says.

The Terror Barrier

Bob Proctor says when you don't break through the terror barrier, you go back into bondage. This means you're still operating from your old paradigms, you're struggling to go forward, and your faith isn't very good. As soon as you completely smash that terror barrier, those chains completely fall away and you're no longer in bondage.

Lloyd says, "There was a time when the thought of me being the only one responsible for how much money was in my bank absolutely terrified me.

"For three-and-a-half years I ran a Direct Sales business. I would go out with the guys training them on residential campaigns. I treated every day like my bank account was at zero and I had to sell to eat."

Because of the nature of the work and the responsibility of training, managing, guiding and in some cases counseling his workforce the hours were very long. The money was great, but it was subject to variable factors.

Eventually, Lloyd just wanted a corporate job so that he could focus on one element. "I was burnt out I think. I did the door to door work initially because I didn't have a job, but when the recession ended I wanted some comfort and returned to the corporate world."

For Lloyd to break through that barrier again and go back to being self-employed was a big deal. "It was why my goal initially had been to become part of a team that was going somewhere, because I didn't believe I could do it. I felt like the world rested on my shoulders and I wasn't ready or willing for the burden. Back then my personal self-image was different from what it is now, and I wasn't ready then."

When Lloyd did *Thinking Into Results*, he abstained from alcohol for a year. "It completely changed my life and my outlook on everything. My focus went from, 'Let's have fun and live it up,' to actually thinking there were things to be done, and a life to be built that didn't revolve around how much fun I could have in the next 25 minutes. As much as I wanted to have fun every 25 minutes, something had to change. My habitual behavior over a 15 or 20-year period was where I was just more interested in having fun than anything of any real value, certainly nothing of service to anybody. That was not on my radar at all. What changed was I realized that all of the things I went through, I went through for the purpose of helping other people."

Listen to Your Intuition – Higher Faculties

Something told Jackie to watch *The Secret*. "Once you get an idea of the little voices that guide you, you realize that you want to do a thing but you don't necessarily know why. I learned to just go with my gut instinct, primarily because I learned that intuition is one of our higher faculties."

Many wonder how to tell the difference between intuition and a paradigm talking to you. It takes a heck of a lot of practice to be able to discern between the two. As you move up the levels of vibration, the more you get to understand this material and how you can change, and how you can tap into these different faculties. As your experience grows, you get to be able to spot the difference between a paradigm talking and the wisdom of your intuition.

"When I was watching *The Secret,* I was absolutely loving it. Bob Proctor was talking about visualization and that if you really want to get emotionally involved in your goals, you have got to be able to see yourself already in them — this is where you talk about living as if," Jackie explains. "He emphasized the importance of really getting connected and actually believing that you are going to attain those goals, that you are attaining those goals."

You must be able to close your eyes and see yourself in the house that you want, and not only see yourself driving but really feeling yourself in the driver's seat of that car you've been eyeing.

"Up to that point, I had tried many times to visualize.

Perhaps because I have so much noise going on in my head or maybe because I'm a very creative person, I find it very, very difficult to sit still. It takes a lot of practice to get a clear picture in my head of the house I want. It's almost like I can't see it in 3D; I can only see it in 2D pictures," Jackie said. "I did my best to visualize but didn't feel I was hitting this mark that Bob Proctor described. My visions were flat. Not coloured, either. And even when I did get started, I couldn't do visualization for very long. Only in little bits here and there. Certainly not enough to change anything.

"So on this particular day, my intuition said to me, 'Jackie, watch *The Secret*. It was fascinating because I watched the movie and the very next day, myself and my husband Shane were sitting on the couch in the lounge. He was flicking back and forth through the channels and I wanted to take that remote and smack him over the head with it. Then he landed on one of the news channels which I wouldn't have been normally watching if I had been alone. I am not a news kind of person.

"And there's Mark Zuckerberg shaking the hand of the Oculus founder after he had just purchased Oculus Rift. Oculus had just come out with a brand new virtual reality system. Virtual reality (VR) has been around for many years but it was a very basic virtual reality. Now they have taken VR into a new playing field altogether. I was watching this and I was seeing the VR games that they were making when this massive eureka moment hit me. A light bulb went off in my head: I could create a virtual reality vision board where people could actually get into their visions! How nice it would be if I could have my vision in VR and be inside my vision so that I didn't have to sit there struggling with my eyes closed. I could have my eyes wide open and be in my vision and actually experience it and then have fun with it and really get emotionally attached to it. I knew I was on to something.

I jumped up and my husband asked, "Where are you going?" I can't remember if I wrote it down or what I did. I just thought, "I have this amazing idea and I have to put it down on paper right this second.

"My personal goal at the time was to have a million in the bank. My money goal was that I wanted to be earning at least a minimum of 5 grand a month. I had a picture on my computer of a million. Every day I would stare at this million. At that stage, I wanted to be successful in marriage. I wanted to be successful in business. I wanted to have my own business and I thought that network marketing was it."

But when this Eureka moment happened to Jackie, it was life-changing. "Everything felt right. I didn't know how I was going to do it but I was going to do it. I knew I was going to find a way. Next, I knew I needed to find the people who could help me do it. When I first told Ewa about the idea, her reaction was, 'That is really good. It's fascinating.' But she then warned me to be careful. She knew of course that I try and do too many things at the same time. That is another paradigm of mine. I am a very creative brain, so I have all these ideas running around my head. Rather than focusing on one thing, making it successful, and then moving on to something else, I can be very scattered.

Chapter 6: Repeat, Repeat, Repeat & Love That Mirror

So what is mirror work?

Mirror work is based on affirmations and constant spaced repetition.

Mirror work is saying affirmations to yourself in the mirror. When you're working on a particular goal and you want something to happen, you can use mirror work to speed up the gestation period of your goal.

You do this by standing before the mirror and reciting your goal three times while looking first into the left eye, and then three times looking into the right.

"Currently I'm working on a weight loss goal," Jackie said. "So I write on my goal card, 'I'm happy and grateful now that it is the 3rd of June in the next year and I'm at 75 kg.' I recite my goal into the mirror as described above, then I put some emotions into it. I give a cheer or a yell. When you first start to do it, it might feel ridiculous but you quickly get used to it."

If you want something to manifest quickly, you can do mirror work on the hour, every waking hour. Jackie says, "I put on an event a few years ago. I was selling Jeunesse products through network marketing and thought of this amazing idea to build confidence using the products. I wanted a stylist to talk to the attendees about how to style yourself to look awesome, no matter what size you are. I got Ewa to talk at the event about self-love, and women and confidence, and things along that line.

I pictured 80 people attending my event. I had spent quite a bit of money putting the show together and I absolutely had to fill those seats."

Mirror work came in when Jackie wondered how she was going to fill the room. "For me to break even I had to get at least 50 people into the room. Before I did the mirror work, it was three weeks out and only 8 tickets had been purchased! I was stressing out!"

Ewa instructed Jackie, "Say into your left eye and into your right eye three times, I'm just happy and grateful now that I see 80 beautiful women in the room all enjoying the event."

She reminded Jackie to put some emotion into it each time. Jackie set her alarm on the hour every hour, performing this sequence of events every single day.

The shift started to occur immediately. Throughout the day, ideas started coming to Jackie about how to fill the room.

"I was contacted by Groupon. I thought that raising money for charity would be a great way to give back. I contacted fashion houses who would promote their clothes and promote the event. All these ideas were amazing," Jackie said.

As Jackie followed through on the suggestions filling her mind, little by little the tickets began to move, and sales multiplied. By the time the event came around, Jackie had 78 women in the room.

The way this works is by doing the affirmations you start to believe that it is 100% possible for your goal to occur. The universe conspires to make it happen. The universe or energy gives you the ideas to make it happen, and then you go out and do so. It's not magic.

Jackie says, "This is where I believe people misunderstand *The Secret* and think 'If I just see myself with money then tomorrow I'll wake up with money in my bank account.' There's a bit more involved here!"

Lloyd affirms that you've got to have faith in order to work with faith. But — and this is important — you have to WORK toward your goal as well as have faith. Without work, what is faith alone? The two together must tie in very nicely.

What happens when you start doing affirmations and then do the mirror work and you say these affirmations over and over, the belief grows exponentially.

Jackie explains that it's an energy ball that continues to grow and expand and before you know it you're getting all these ideas you wonder why you never thought of before!

The mind is incredibly powerful. Mind work is what really makes the difference.

Using mirror work, Lloyd attracted a very distinct type of job to himself. "One of the things that I wanted in my life was to start in a company that was in the very early stages. I wanted to build up that company and be part of a team because I didn't yet have the confidence to believe I could do it on my own. It sounded intimidating to figure out some idea, and even if I had the right idea would I have the revenue? I wanted then to be part of a team that already had the revenue and market validation, so I could focus on my area of expertise."

Lloyd thought about this goal every day. "I wrote it down on a piece of paper and did the mirror work every day. I got a message on LinkedIn from a company in Argentina, which read, "We've got a client who is interested in interviewing you."

When Lloyd asked who they were, he wasn't told. "I said I didn't want to be interviewed by someone when I didn't even know who they were! They hadn't told me anything really, not how much money I was going to get, what was the offer, or even what part of the world it was in."

He agreed to the interview anyway and recognized the speaker was from somewhere in North Africa, and that English wasn't his first language. He spoke French, with an

American accent. "As I tried to figure out his origins, I wondered about this country or that country. Who was this guy? He interviewed me a couple of times on Skype and I still didn't know what the job was, or who he was, or anything else. It was just totally bizarre."

Eventually, the speaker asked Lloyd to research a particular market industry and get back to him with industry norms areas where Lloyd identified potential growth. "At the time I was working in a company as a market research reseller. We didn't do custom research, and I wasn't an analyst. I was working as a salesman and now this man was asking me to break down the whole industry. Clearly, this was a test."

Lloyd had the feeling that this opportunity could be the job he had been visualizing. "A friend of mine is a marketing director who studied marketing for 4 years in university. I did not; I ran a door to door sales and marketing company. This was not the same thing as somebody who is educated on the business side of marketing. There were lots of things like growth hacking that I wasn't familiar with; there were all sorts of confusing questions."

Lloyd rang his friend and said, "I need to send you something. I have no idea what this guy is talking about. None. Please, can you have a look at these questions and tell me where to look? Can you send me a couple of links of relevance that I can research so I can make a coherent answer for this guy?"

The friend agreed.

"I didn't have an offer yet, so this exercise was for him to see what I was capable of putting together on the spot. Due to my friend's significant contribution, I managed to pull together a report that took me about 20 hours. Now if I hadn't been doing the mind work, and this opportunity — for me to move to another country, run a company from scratch as a marketing director while having no experience in marketing whatsoever — had appeared, I would never have entertained the email in the first place," Lloyd explains.

Lloyd sent the report and the response was overwhelmingly positive. "Simon, our CEO, said, 'Wow this is amazing. This is spot on. I am so impressed right now!' Meanwhile, I was thinking to myself, 'Please don't ask me any questions outside of what you've asked because everything I know is on that piece of paper.' And at last, he offered me the position of Marketing Director of a high-potential startup in Santiago, Chile. They covered my flights and estimated I would be down there in about 6 weeks. So, I quit my job and got on a plane to South America. As it happened, I surprised myself and it seems that it was really my self-belief that needed to grow.

One of the things Simon said to Lloyd was, "I can tell that you're the type of person who likes all your ducks in a row."

Lloyd replied, "'Yes, I do, I like structure.' I'm not actually very structured as a human being but I like structure because it helps me to focus on things. I'm a very strategic person, so it's very rare for me to do anything without 2 or 3 good reasons. I just don't operate any other way."

Next Simon said to Lloyd, "Look, you have to learn something and you're going to work with me on this one. It's called progress over perfection."

Lloyd didn't know what he was talking about. "I didn't even understand what that meant because in my mind perfection is the only option. Anything less than that is a waste of time. However, I concluded after nine months in Chile that in fact progress over perfection was the only way to build a startup because each of us had to do 8 or 9 jobs at the same time. We often had to do an en*TIR*e day's work in an hour and then change to a different role in the same company and do it again for another hour, and then do that in another hour — 8–10 hours a day.

"The workload was alarming. Each day I needed to write a blog post. The posts were on multiple research reports within a market segment. I wrote each post from scratch, from the idea of the concept to the whole structure written with links to individual research reports that we had on our website. These posts had to be researched, written, proofread, and posted on our internal blog within 55 minutes every day of the week!

"At one point, Simon said he thought I could easily write 3 posts in an hour and I told him I couldn't possibly do that. I said if he wanted it to be good, that's just not going to work. But he insisted, and I actually did manage to write a blog post in 25 minutes and post it, and it was the best blog I'd ever written. I wrote it in 25 minutes, but I nearly had a nervous breakdown while I was doing it. Simon asked me to do that again.

"Another time I had to create 13 press releases in an hour, then the next hour I had to write a blog and after that, I created a list of 500 procurement managers to send a bulk email to on a particular research report in a particular industry. It was insane, like, really off-the-wall level of productivity," Lloyd says.

I have to say despite the workload I owe Simon a lot for his mentorship. I learned a lot and we were seeing success in a very competitive market. But my relationship was suffering with me being so far away, so I decided to make the move to Ireland.

Lloyd said at the time that he had no doubt the en*TIR*e opportunity arose because of his mind and mirror work.

"When I arrived home, I decided to work for myself. Since then I have launched 3 other businesses in Ireland. Thanks to my mirror work I created the opportunity to move to South America and the courage to act on the impulse. I wanted to move to another country with a hot climate, I wanted to do it in a startup company, I wanted to learn new skills, I wanted to learn how a business starting from very early stages can make all those things happen. I truly believe that if I hadn't been thinking about all that, how could I have had an imagination big enough to entertain that email and end up in Santiago, Chile."

The synchronicity continued. "As it transpired, my girlfriend broke up with me the day after I got back from Chile. But I needed to be in Ireland to meet another key individual, who ironically enough had introduced me to Jackie almost 2 years previously. Eric is the gentleman who I went into business with when I got off the plane. I would have never met Jackie if not for Eric, and if not for me being in South America and coming back for my ex-girlfriend who broke up with me, I never would have been in Ireland to have a conversation with Eric, to go into business with Eric, and finally wouldn't have gotten to do the book or course with Jackie. There's quite a lot of things tied together."

Chapter 7: Getting All Scientific in Here

"The feeling is the secret."

—Neville Goddard

Up until now, you've probably thought of emotion and intuition and science to be separate from one another, but recent discoveries in modern science and quantum physics have turned a lot of this on its head.

So now we are going to get a bit 'Sciencey' here.

Emotion and Intuition

In 1991 scientists discovered 40,000 specialized cells called 'sensory neurites' in the human heart. They are like brain cells, but they are not in the brain. They think independent of the brain and head, they feel independent of the brain and head, and they remember independent of the brain and head.

The heart communicates with the brain in 4 ways:

- Neurological communication (nervous system)
- Biochemical communication (hormones)
- Biophysical communication (pulse wave)
- Energetic communication (electromagnetic fields)

Aside from having an intrinsic nervous system independent of the central nervous system, more communication travels from heart to brain than the other way around. Our brain has an electromagnetic field as well as an electrical field.

These cells in the heart do too, but the electromagnetic fields are 500 times stronger and the electrical fields are 100 times stronger.

In the folklore of the Cherokee tribe, this was called *chante ishta*: the single eye of the heart.

With visualization and manifestation, once we marry the two, starting in the heart with gratitude we can more quickly attract our desired results by applying the Law of Visualization.

Three-Step Process

Step 1. Touch your heart center gently, in a way that is comfortable to you. Your awareness will always go to the place on your body where you feel the touch.
Mayan people do this with the flat of their hand as do the people of the middle east. Buddhists make the symbol for prayer two hands together and then press to the heart.

You are sending a signal to your body that you are sending awareness inside rather than outside.

Step 2. Begin to breathe a little slower. This replicates the heart rate of when you are in a place of safety. This will turn off the adrenal/cortisol response of fight and flight and open up powerful immune responses.

Step 3. Begin to feel (to the best of your ability) your way from heart to brain. There are some very powerful word concepts in the English language that allow us to connect to this emotion.

They are APPRECIATION, GRATITUDE, COMPASSION, and CARE.

This signal is at a very low frequency, optimized at 0.1Hz well below the DELTA frequency.

This is the frequency where whales communicate in the ocean.

This is the power of our heart.

This is called heart-brain coherence and the conversation is determined by our emotions.

If we choose the emotion we can choose/change the conversation which determines the hormonal chemistry that the heart releases into the body. Once we are in this space, this is how we heal ourselves, this is how we access our intuition.

We all have an infinite source of supply, intelligence and wisdom accessed through this single eye of the heart. It is said prayers are not answered while you are praying, they are answered while you are listening for the answer to your prayers.

Once you tap into the power of the heart, its magnetic link to the thinking substance, its electrical link to the atoms in your body and around you, to intuition, to your vision, you will begin to understand why contemplation and calm are so important.

Your emotions control the conversation between heart and mind. This is key to visualization.

We know from Thomas Troward, Geneviève Behrend, and others that the only way to magnetize our vision and goal into our material reality is to hold it on the screen of our mind, use affirmations to communicate directly to the universe vibrationally, and to focus on the result as a completely natural thing that already exists in our life now that we are hugely grateful for.

For example, when she went through *Thinking Into Results* a second time, Jackie realized she had undergone a lot of changes around her feelings. "I definitely felt my outlook had improved massively. I understood the difference between conscious and subconscious thinking and how you can actually change your habits and focus. One of my main things was trying to shift my health and weight. There was definitely a click happening there and I think that was very, very important."

She finally understood an important concept at a very deep level. "It was as if someone said to me, 'Look, you've got to start taking control — because you really are your own creation. You create everything that is around you. You create your life and everything in it with your thoughts and feelings.'"

While speaking with a friend, Jackie said that she'd love a house in Florida. "I always wanted to live somewhere nice and warm. I love Florida because it's not too far from Europe, but it's in America, and I love America. It's big and money flows freely and the people are amazing and it's very like South Africa. So I said to my friend, 'I want a house in Florida on the beach. It's really easy to fly to Europe so people can come to me. Florida is fabulous.'"

The friend replied, "Jackie you're going to be living in a house in Florida in the next couple of years because everything you say, you do!"

"I've only just realized lately how strong my ability to create the world around me is," Jackie says. "But this goes both ways, positive and negative. For example, there was an instance where I was supposed to host an online meeting with a couple of people for my business. I wondered to myself what would happen if no one came to the meeting? I realized that I would love a break, just a passing thought really. But guess what happened? Not one person showed up to the online meeting! I had to laugh because even though I wanted a break, I was annoyed that I was sitting in front of the computer staring at an empty zoom meeting room. I still chuckle at this today."

Every time a negative thought pops into Jackie's head, she takes action. "I think, 'Cancel!' My intuition has grown very strong, but I think it's become a lot stronger since my faith in myself has grown. Ever since I've proven to people that I could get the investments for *Genie in a Headset*, I think my awareness has grown even more. I've changed frequencies and raised my level of vibration and that's why I get how people say that the law of attraction is so magical."

Jackie used to question herself all the time because she didn't have a lot of self-confidence. "I questioned what I was thinking and felt I was clearly not good enough. So even though I had strong intuition, I used to dismiss it. I let myself down in a lot of areas because my self-image was not as strong as it is now. I didn't have confidence in myself and my ability. Now I can say, yes, I do have very strong intuition. I actually listen to that little voice and I know the difference between intuition and gremlins."

Bob Proctor told Jackie that after studying and doing *Thinking Into Results*, she would need a telescope to look back at herself. "He was right. I need two telescopes now if I want to look back at how far I've come. I get that now. If I didn't decide that I wanted to make my vision a reality and submit it to *Voom*, if I didn't get Lloyd to do the video, all of these other things wouldn't be happening because the ball wouldn't have started rolling. Because of that video we made, the idea became something more than the idea in my head because it actually looked good and sounded good in the video."

Lloyd explains the miracle from his point of view. "I had spoken to a lady called Lisa White who asked me to pitch the idea of making the video to a business associate of hers. This other woman was very impressed and asked me to make a video for their company. This inspired me to get a business plan together. Jackie that evening on the very same day asked me to make her video. I didn't miss the coincidence." Ironically, that other video never got made — but it put the idea on my radar and so I was open to Jackie's idea, otherwise it may never have happened.

Lloyd is a strong believer in the connections between people and things. "It's very interesting how things come full circle. Now everything I do, and everywhere I look all the dots are connecting. It's like a thread of a very big pattern of which I am the center. I remember reading this book years ago called *The Wheel of Time*. There's a world and everybody's life was a single string and the world was wound together into a pattern and it's called the pattern of the universe. So it's quite interesting how that pattern is tying itself around people's desire and people's emotion and drive and passion and vision."

"Just think about how many people have been influenced by Steve Jobs' vision. He's only one guy. So there are people that come along and simply realize that they're in a pattern and that they have the ability to influence that pattern. They're the change makers, they're the visionaries, they're the ones who make it all happen," Lloyd says.

Lloyd never had a lack of faith in himself in terms of his ability. "I had a lack of faith in my discipline because I had created some very unconstructive habits over the years. Breaking away from that was something that was necessary for me to realize my full potential. Up until that point I'd never applied myself nor made a solid effort to realize my true potential. Everyone I have come into contact with has been telling me since I was 4 years old that I was going to do something very special in this world, so I just took it for granted it was going to happen without me actually doing anything. It turned out that what they really meant was, 'Lloyd, you have a lot of potential to do good things in the world as long you don't intentionally waste all of your time on absolute trivia.'"

When Lloyd looked at whatever they were talking about in terms of his paradigm, and his habitual behavior, he realized all the best parts of his paradigm came from his family. "The worst parts were all mine and I was fully aware that I created that paradigm. Through association and through desire to not conform for whatever reason I had a lot of things to undo in order to become successful," Lloyd admits. "Now in a majority of cases, I'm free to shine like I should have in the first place. There was a long time when that wasn't happening. Visualizing myself as a person who deserved to succeed by his actions as opposed to deserved by his perceived self-image was where the issue was. It just felt like so many opportunities were there for me and I wasted them or missed them altogether.

"When Jackie and I agreed to make her video, I was thinking that somebody wanted me to do something of value, so I was going to go and do it. I didn't think any further than that, really. I was at a point where in my professional career it had been a while since anybody paid me to create, as opposed to paying me for hours and service." Lloyd had been in sales for a long time, so he was really excited about the idea of bringing together and marrying all the skill sets he had developed up until that point in order to create something new.

His training in video production and direction under his brother's expert guidance gave him the necessary confidence to pursue the idea and produce the movie for Jackie.

Equally, Lloyd has always been a good writer and as a young man it looked like he might pursue such a career but like most things the naysayers have a habit of knocking the wind out of our sails unless we have the tenacity to persevere or the guidance of a good mentor. While working in Chile, he had to write blogs about industries that he knew nothing about and pull it together in 45 minutes, then add reports and industry statistics. "So I got into a groove where I knew that it didn't matter what the topic was or which industry — I could write it." This act of creation gave Lloyd the confidence he needed to have a conversation with Jackie about partnering with her to create their course and this book.

"One of the things I recognized was that there was a reason why I decided that I would be recording the video. I studied theater, and I've been acting for the camera, and I've been to America to pursue an acting career. I've also been in sales for years. I had a keen interest in video as my brother makes films and promotional videos for social partnerships in the

UK, through his company *Be Inspired Films,* Lloyd was looking at what he could do that could help him to create a career outside of sales.

Lloyd's brother, Ravinol, also teaches a course called VideoKnowHow — which Lloyd had just finished in preparation for his new career outside of sales. "One of the main focuses is teaching people how to create a narrative for their business and their journey and their mission that others can buy into. Personally, I was really interested in startups because at the time I was working in a building with a lot of startups called the Guinness Enterprise Centre in Dublin, which is a startup support ecosystem like a new business accelerator. Ironically, I found out a long time later that Jackie's husband actually has been running a business from the GEC the whole time, without us ever bumping into one another there."

In this ecosystem, founders go through a process of getting funding, building their startup business, and market validation. They can then base their SME at the GEC renting small places specifically for startups.

Lloyd was working on a couple of ideas at the time. The first was a holistic website based around helping the public source holistic practitioners online around Dublin. The second was to make promotional videos for startup companies. The second idea won out in the end.

Lloyd's focus was always on the little guy. "I liked the energy of new ideas in their infancy, and I wanted to help them get themselves out there so they could make their dreams happen. My impulse was that people deserved to dream, and people deserved to have a life more than they had. If I could help people do that, by creating a narrative people could get behind and relate to — well that's a great way to make a living. It's in an industry where I had access to a lot of expertise, yet I didn't need much initial outlay."

Lloyd actively uses his intuition now but at the time intuition was not a concept he was comfortable with or took very seriously. "Now, I talk to people about feeling and emotion but at the time there was little to no chance of me having those kinds of conversations. I think as a female those conversations are more acceptable. As a male, it's not a conversation that you often have."

When Jackie and Lloyd discussed making the video, he was thinking from a business perspective. Jackie had the idea and Lloyd had the necessary level of belief and faith in the world of ideas to help turn it from an idea into a great video for her to promote.

A, B, and C Type Goals

At that point, Lloyd wondered about Jackie's goal and how he could categorize it?

An A-Type Goal is doing something you already know how to do. Say you have a four-year-old Mustang GT500. You bought it new four years prior. Your goal is to buy a new Mustang GT500, so you buy that car. There is no growth in this, as you have known for 4 years how to do this.

A B-Type Goal is what you think you can and are qualified to do. You interview for a new job because, after reading the job advertisement, you know you have the experience to get that particular job.

A C-Type Goal is based on fantasy as, if money and time were not an issue, what would you do? Here is where you ask yourself what you want? What are your big fantasy goals?

Starting your own business is a C-type goal, but learning a new skill and getting a new job is a B-type goal. Jackie was working with a true C-type goal, and Lloyd knew he wanted to get behind brave people, not recognizing himself yet to be one of those people. "I didn't see myself as a visionary, but I had faith anyway. So when Jackie came to me and said she was interested in making a video and was looking for somebody who was great with words with a sales mindset, I was probably thinking that I was going to make money. I already knew how to do sales, so the idea just fit me. This was an idea that was so big, I figured we could make the video and then figure it out."

Lloyd's time in Chile learning how to make things happen with very little revenue would stretch his visualization and imagination. "We were trying so many different strategies to get the mix right with very few resources, as money was very tight. While working in that startup I was being paid through funding, it wasn't through revenue. All the people were giving their time or they were bootstrapping, and every penny was going back into development and marketing. They all had other businesses, they were only giving 10–15 hours a week, and the CEO was bootstrapping from his own cash because he had consulting work on the side."

"I still do listen to a lot of Pink Floyd and I didn't want to be another brick in the wall with a face strapped on. I had always wanted to go and do my own thing but I never had any idea where to start." Thankfully everything happened the way it did and Lloyd is eternally grateful for how his partnership with Jackie has turned out.

"It's so empowering to see the universe willing to receive and graciously give," Lloyd says. "I learned a lot of discipline in Chile so when I got back and talked to Jackie, I was thinking maybe I'll do more videos and wondered if she needed another video. You know 80% of your sales come from existing customers."

From a sales point of view, contacting Jackie was an obvious place to start. There was talk of Jackie putting together a course about visualization to help as many people as possible to understand and learn the exciting concepts she had discovered, and there was a book which had been started too.

Lloyd suggested to partner up. Jackie got the contracts drawn up and they began to create together. "I had recently started a career in network marketing. This meant my obligations weren't full-time, so I had some spare time and was open. Isn't that interesting?"

What a pleasure it has been!

Chapter 8: Living in the Clouds

> *"Look at your feet. You are standing in the sky. When we think of the sky, we tend to look up, but the sky actually begins at the earth."*
>
> —*Diane Ackerman*

While Jackie didn't meet her goal of being selected for *VOOM*, did that mean she failed?

No!

It didn't matter at all because a new plan was set into action.

It merely differed in appearance, but it was every bit as viable.

Is that my ride?

The key takeaway from this part of the story is to recognize that the chariot you envision to make your dream a reality may differ in appearance when it arrives. Once Jackie and Lloyd created the video, the Genie moved closer to becoming a reality.

Without the time pressure of the *Voom* Awards, Jackie doesn't think she could have (or would have) gotten the ball rolling. "My having to pull it all together in a week gave the Genie the momentum it needed to travel along the path to manifestation. If I hadn't put together the pitch, and started visualizing all the things that needed creation around the pitch, it might still otherwise be me thinking about it, rather than putting finishing touches to it."

We are all familiar with the New Year goals that well-meaning folks around the world set for themselves.

Lloyd recently asked a friend about his goals for the upcoming year. "He gave me a list of 25 different things, and when he was finished I said those are plans, they are not goals. They sound nice and I hope you do them all, but they don't constitute goals. A goal is something you've never done before. And if it doesn't scare you and excite you at the same time then it's not big enough."

When you set a goal, you don't need to know how it's going to happen. Just set it and forget it. This same friend told Lloyd that he didn't want to limit his goals to a single year. Lloyd agreed that you limit your goals in general by placing them inside of a year. "Who is to decide what can be achieved in a year? When I look back at where I was a year ago there is no comparison. I don't even see the same person, the same life, or anything else. In terms of how much potentiality there is, it can't be confined to a timeline.

The Importance of Making Decisions

The Genie happened because Jackie made the decision to commission the video. Decision making is about exercising a muscle. You're not good or bad at decision making, but you do develop a skill from doing it more often. You exercise the muscle called decision making.

Lloyd says, "Personally, I pick things I want to achieve and I make a decision to succeed whether it's pleasant or not. Successful people are motivated by pleasing results while everyone else is motivated by pleasing methods. Just like with hard work, once you create a habit around your actions they become effortless."

Sometimes that means creating a habit out of doing things that failures don't like to do. That's the price of success. You've heard this before. Lloyd follows through on whatever the decision he's made regardless of consequences or circumstances and when it is no longer convenient because that is what is required.

Jackie's decision to create the Genie was a great idea and so she made the decision to make the video. In doing so, she learned what was predicted for the market.

"If people can predict the market then I can predict my future," Jackie decided. At the time, she was in the process of learning the universal laws. "We were assigned to understand them, and I don't think we understood them anywhere near what we do now. But certainly, I had the beginnings of understanding the potential to manifest anything we want in the universe. It was becoming clear to me, like a cloud-parting."

Jackie was brave enough to make the decision to create the video and Lloyd happened to be in her life at the same time. "Since we work so very well together anyway, we were off! That's how the video came to be," Lloyd explains.

"We uploaded the video onto a platform and then shared the platform around to everybody we knew for them to vote us in," Jackie explained. "We wanted to get in front of the panel of experts but we were limited by time. Still, it was definitely a brilliant process to initiate because it pushed the Genie a lot further down the path toward existence."

During this time Jackie's husband Shane turned to her and asked, "What are you doing with that picture on your phone?" Jackie had created a screensaver where she put her face onto another woman sitting next to Richard Branson. "People are going to think you're a stalker!" Shane said. "Will you get that off your phone?"

"I still have it, which is mental, but I just have this feeling that I will be meeting Richard Branson someday very soon," Jackie says.

"Or perhaps he will be meeting you?" Lloyd suggests.

The video was shot in one day, edited in three, and ready to post in seven days. Once created, the video had its own path toward bringing all these other things into existence that hadn't existed before. Lloyd explains, "It's the concept that what you want, wants you. So once you birth an idea, then the idea has its own energy. You become grateful for the idea that has used you."

The moment you think of an idea, it has its own energy and its en*TIR*e goal is to be actualized. "When Jackie had that idea about the Genie, it existed from that moment on. It's a global first-in-class, it was the first time anybody made an interactive virtual reality game that rewards positive self-development activities within a game. It has never been done before. So the moment that she had the idea, that existed in its en*TIR*ety. All of its energy was focused on coming into being," Lloyd says.

The rest of it was always going to come together. "It was always going to happen from the moment she had the idea. Then she made a decision, and once you make a decision, and you set the goal it's not possible or probable: it's inevitable. All you have to do is not quit. That's it. Everything else is set. If you do quit, your idea will find somebody else and make it happen because it wants to happen."

The concept of an idea "using" a person to be born is not a new one. Let's say you write a book, or create a work of art, or design a new business concept. Once they come into being, they each take on existences of their own. It's similar to birthing a child. You have this child, and you raise them, but they will also be their own entity with their own thoughts, desires and life plans. They're not "yours." Creative works are exactly the same. You are the vehicle that brings them into existence, yet they have an existence separate from you.

"Interestingly, a limited liability company works the same way," Lloyd explains. "Although the company is made by the director, he or she could be fired or die and yet the company still exists. It doesn't cease to exist because the host or the originator does. The company can go into liquidation and yet the director can still be alive. The company can owe a lot of money and cease to exist, yet because there's limited liability the director can just walk away."

The Principle of Agreed Imagined Reality

If everybody agrees on the same thing it seems to be true at a glance, but this has nothing to do with truth. Just because everybody agrees on something, that doesn't make it true: it's just agreed imagined reality.

Ideas are the precursor to this. Similarly, just because everyone says something can't be true doesn't have anything to do with whether it is or not. All new ideas that challenge current norms must overcome this. As creators, we become the vehicle for bringing these ideas to form.

Jackie wanted to write a book. Jackie wanted to design and deliver an online course. Jackie thought of the Genie. Jackie wanted to make a video. "I said I would help her make the video and we did so," Lloyd explains. "Jackie went off to do her thing, I was off to another part of the world. I returned and agreed to write the book with her. Then she wanted to create a course. Next thing I had an epiphany and a structure came together for the course to happen in all of 18 seconds."

The structure of the book grew up around what Jackie had given Lloyd to work with, but the course structure came straight from the ether!

The actual process of the creative part of the idea coming in happened so quickly. Lloyd explains, "Obviously we have developed a lot since then, but a couple of months ago it was also just an idea. Jackie mentioned that she was thinking about a course and now we have a fully functioning course. That course has already been introduced to the world. We have taken 2 paid groups through it already and it is going to change many lives — and it took just 18 seconds to be born."

Lloyd has been writing poetry and songs since he was about 11 years old. "I always had this knowledge that when it hits you, you have to be ready. I used to have a pen and paper beside my bed. When an idea hit me in the night I would roll over and write it down and go back to sleep. Now I use my phone. I have 25 different business ideas on my phone. They come to me all the time, and so I imagine other people must get them all the time too."

If this is so, naturally one wonders what people do with their ideas? Ask people what they want and they'll tell you, "I don't have a goal." Lloyd says he doesn't believe that. "I believe people often do know what they want. They just discount it before the idea is fully formed. In other words, you have an idea and you don't allow it to be born."

Jackie believes people block themselves because of low self-esteem, noticing that once her self-image changed, her life changed. "I think when people get an idea they often get an automatic response from their paradigm. They hear: that idea will never work. I don't think that they think it will never work, I believe their self-image of who they think they are is so ingrained that they don't even notice the paradigm is doing the speaking."

Jackie mentions that in Dr. Maxwell Maltz's *Psycho-Cybernetics* he talked about how we do not tend to realize how deeply rooted our self-image and confidence is. We automatically behave the way we do, say the things we say, and act the way we act because of our self-image. If a person wants to see a change in results, they have to change the way they see themselves.

Lloyd agrees. "When we discount an idea before it's fully formed, we often do that innately. If you're not in control, then something else is because someone's got to be in control. In other words, if you're not directing the flow, then you're going with the flow. Ever ask yourself — then who is directing the flow?"

Jackie feels that we operate from our level of awareness. This influences how we operate and direct results around us. The more our awareness levels grow, the more powerful we become. Jackie made sure to emulate this concept with the Genie. "In the game, your awareness bar gets bigger and bigger if you do all of these amazing little exercises the Genie instructs you to do. While you're passing time on your amazing island in the sun where you have a beautiful villa, you can go and have a look at your vision board in virtual reality and see which piece you would like to manifest this week. Once your awareness bar gets bigger and brighter, then you will know you're on the right track."

It's very much the same in real life. You grow your awareness by taking classes such as *Thinking Into Results*, or attending seminars like *The Matrixx*, or getting in touch with Bob Proctor and the Proctor Gallagher Institute, or attending one of Tony Robbins' programs. "It's all about self-study and growing your level of awareness," Jackie says.

Lloyd recounts an incident at one of Ewa's events. There was a 14-year-old boy from Moldova who attended her event to find out about how to make worthy goals. When Ewa asked, "Who has a goal? Who's willing to share?" this boy put up his hand.

Ewa said that she'd received an email from his mother asking if he was old enough to attend the event.

"I wrote that email," the boy confessed. His goal was to make his mother proud because he said she was an outside-the-box thinker, but his grandmother thought all this stuff was a load of nonsense. He wanted to impress his very forward-thinking mother. It was established that he shouldn't be taking the course for his mother.

Ewa instructed him to by all means go accomplish things, but don't do it just to make her proud. She will be proud anyway. Nowadays we have access to so much more knowledge than even 10 years ago but that being said for a boy that age to make a decision to move in that direction, he is already at a level of awareness where he could recognize that personal growth is an important part of life. It meant his mindset was that improvements could be made.

Once you get to a point where you recognize that there's a progression level in your awareness, you realize you are in control of how it works from that point. You recognize that you have a part to play in your advancement from a personal development perspective. Lloyd says, "I nearly had tears in my eyes, which is very unusual for me. There were women crying all over the place at this amazing boy's actions!"

Because Jackie got an idea, she made a decision to take action. Although the goal was to score high enough in the *Voom* competition, it turned out that the competition was only the vehicle for bringing the video into existence. Not winning the competition did not matter in the least, as a new path was forged for the Genie to come to life.

How many times in your life have you felt like you failed because you didn't hit your goal? Did you ever consider that the new path set out to meet your goal might be better?

Chapter 9: Becoming Magnetic

Lloyd has heard Bob Proctor say that if the dream is big enough the facts don't matter. "I believe that. In fact, he also says that once you make a decision, all the money, people, and resources you need will turn up, attracted to your vibration of thought. I have known about that for a long time, but it wasn't until we looked back on this process that we realize that's exactly what happened. It's so inspiring to think that this can work for anyone, because before we set this in motion we were just two average people. It's amazing what a difference a definite purpose can make to your life.

Jackie and Lloyd would like to share a few examples of normal people doing extraordinary things.

Peggy McColl

Peggy McColl is a *New York Times* Best Selling author, international best seller, and Amazon best seller.

I was in a marriage that was changing form and becoming a divorce. My husband and I had a young son who was a baby at the time when we put our house on the market.

Bob Proctor has taught me to use a goal card almost 40 years ago now, so it's a technique that I have used multiple times. Immediately I created a goal card where I wrote a description of the kind of home that I would own next:

"I am so happy and grateful now that I own my beautiful home with 4 bedrooms, 3 bathrooms, a double car garage, in a beautiful community for my son and I, where we could go for walks in the woods and trails where we could ride our bikes."

Charles (my first husband) and I put our house on the market and we weren't getting any action whatsoever. No visitors at all. At the time it was a very depressed real estate market and part of the reason was that some political things were going on at the time. We lived in a province of Quebec that was threatening to separate from Canada, so any English-speaking people were just clearing out of the province. It was just like this mass exodus along the 401 — with everyone heading west out of Quebec.

A lot of people couldn't sell their homes, which was one of the challenges. The other challenge was that the home we owned was in the country which typically has a longer sales cycle because they are not seen as desirable in real estate. I didn't allow that to stand in my way, as that is a condition I don't have any control over.

What I did was to see my son and myself in our beautiful home, which was beautifully decorated. I saw it in my mind's eye even though I didn't know exactly what it would look like, but I saw us enjoying quality time in our neighborhood and playing at the nearby park.

Months and months went by, and we still had no activity on our house. We dropped our price a couple of times, but still nothing.

I would go look at new home showrooms, where builders would showcase new homes and in new subdivisions. On weekends they would hold open houses where you could go and see houses for sale. I would go actively looking and looking and looking.

One day I heard about this draw called the CHEO (Children's Hospital of Eastern Ontario) — the CHEO dream of a lifetime home lottery. How it worked was that you could buy a $100 ticket for this lottery. The prize was a furnished and decorated home that came with a whole bunch of other things, such as top upgrades.

It was open 7 days a week and you could go in and buy your tickets right in the home. I found out where it was, and I drove down the street and as I was driving down the street I could see this park and at the end of the street, there were all these trails. I realized this is exactly what I had visualized, even though I had never seen it before. So, it's like the vision became the reality — here it was.

I pulled into the driveway in front of the double car garage. Inside the home had four bedrooms and three bathrooms, and it was beautifully decorated and designed and it was fully furnished. I knew this was it!

I changed my goal card and on the goal card I added the specific address and wrote, "I, Peggy McColl, am so happy and grateful that I own my beautiful home and am living at (and I put the address down)."

Because that home was open 7 days a week, you could go in there and visit it at any time. They didn't stop you at the door and say, "Wait a minute you were in here yesterday," so I went to visit that home multiple times. I wouldn't just go in the home to take a look around casually, I would drive into the driveway as if I was driving home. I would walk up the front step as if I was coming home. I would imagine putting the key in the door and going into my home. I would walk in and actually sit on the furniture and feel the furniture. I would imagine my son and I in the family room watching a Disney movie on our TV. Then I would go and sit in the kitchen and there would be a woman there who would be selling tickets and I would sit with her at the kitchen table. I would look out the window and think, "Oh this is what it's going to be like when we live here." I would imagine that she was visiting me. Of course, she didn't know what was going on as this whole activity was happening in my mind. Then I would go and sit at the dining room table and I would sit at the head of the table and I would imagine my family was there and we were having our Christmas dinner. I could smell the turkey and I would just have the whole experience. Then I would go into the formal drawing room and I would sit down and imagine us after dinner and having tea or coffee or drinks and then I would go upstairs where the bedrooms were. I chose which room would be my son's room. I had these two guest rooms and they were beautifully decorated and I saw my mom and dad and sister coming to visit. I walked down the hall to the master suite and I laid on the bed. They had this big, wooden sleigh bed and it was so gorgeous and unique. I would lay on the bed and I would look up at the ceiling and I would imagine waking up in the morning and that's what I would see and when I would go to sleep at night that's the last thing I would see before I closed my eyes. I would walk into the en-suite bathroom and imagine that I was getting ready in the morning. It had a big Roman tub, with a separate shower but it had this big roman tub and I jumped in the bath. Now I didn't fill it with water or anything, I just jumped in the tub and put my arms back, closed my eyes and I imagined having a bubble bath. I would smell the bath salts.

It was a whole visualization experience and I didn't do it once, I did it many, many, many times. The girl who was selling tickets got to know me. I just started visualizing, visualizing, visualizing myself living in this home. I bought the ticket a couple months before the draw, so I had a lot of time to really see us living in that home and then the draw came on December 7th.

Doctor John Goodman won the house.

I didn't win the house.

A lot of people think that when I start to tell that story that it will end with me winning the house.

I have learned that when we want something, want to do something, or be something, we set the objective. We see ourselves in the possession of the goods that we desire, or doing what it is we want, or having what it is we want. But we must detach from the outcome and meaning. You can have an unhealthy attachment and if it doesn't happen you will be devastated because that's negative energy.

So when that happened I thought, "Oh, isn't that interesting, maybe it's not that house, but I am not going to throw my goal away." There is that expression not to throw the baby out with the bath water. So that experience happened, and I decided it is what it is, I still have the goal to own a home and I am not going to let go of it. Maybe it's not that house.

So I still had my goal card but I just removed the address on the card so it read, "I Peggy McColl am so happy and grateful that I live in my own home."

A few months went by and the thing with goals is that we set a date for when we are going to realize our goal, as Bob has taught us. We are guessing at best. We don't know when it is going to happen. We can't force the universe to make things happen. There is a law of gestation that dictates that there is a period of time that will elapse before all things will manifest into form. With some things we know what the gestation period is, like a baby. We don't know what the gestation period for certain goals will be.

I didn't know what it was for my house and in the meantime, the house that I was living in with Charles still did not sell. So a few months after the December draw, my son and I went to visit my brother for the weekend. I woke up in the middle of the night and sat bolt upright. I heard this message which sort of came into my consciousness and the message was "go to the house!" I am not one of these psychic people who talk to the dead or anything like that. But this message was so clear and so vivid. I knew exactly what the message was. And intuitively I knew it meant the dream home.

While driving home the next day we had to exit off the highway to go to the neighborhood where the house was. It wasn't our normal route home. As we are driving along the street I can see a FOR SALE sign on the lawn of the home! I figure that's a sign for me.

Now you must understand that I didn't have any money to buy a house. I know we don't need the money because we don't have to know how it's going to happen, we just need to decide we want it. So, I decided that I was going to buy the house. I wrote down the name of the realtor and his phone number and I decided that I was going to go and see that house. Now I had been in that house a hundred times when I was doing that visualization and I knew exactly what that house looked like.

I went over to my friend's, who lived near that house in the neighborhood, and I told them I was going to book an appointment to go and see it. My friend asked, "Why are you bothering the realtor? You have no money and you have already seen that house." I replied that the realtor didn't know that.

So I booked the appointment and my friend and I visited the house the next day. As soon as the realtor put the key in the lock, I was back in my imagination and seeing myself at my house. It wasn't him unlocking the door — it was me unlocking the door and they were coming into my home. I stepped into my imagination and I also paid attention to how it intuitively felt in the home.

Did I really want it? Was this somewhere I would want to live? Could I see me and my son living there? And there was a strong YES. The confirmation was very clear that absolutely this was the home that I would love to own and live in.

I left there determined to find a way to own that home. I called the realtor a couple of days later and asked for a second visit. That's very common for people in real estate to go back and visit the house again. This time I brought my son because I wanted to see him running around the hall, as he was two and a half at the time. I went back to see the house, and my son was running around and looking around the rooms and that really helped solidify my vision. Then a day later I was driving by the house again, almost to the point of stalking the house! By the way, Dr. John Goodman won the house but didn't need it. He already had a house and furniture, so all the furniture that came with the house was still inside.

I was listening to some cassettes and Tony Robbins was talking about *The Philosophy of Stretching* and he said the following, "The Philosophy of Stretching is when you think you can't, you must. Not for what you get but for who you become."

That was it. I grabbed my cell phone and called the realtor and I said I wanted to make an offer. An idea just came to me, straight into my consciousness. I said, "I am in front of the house, parked on the street right now." He drove over to the house and we sat at the dining room table.

I said, "Here is what I am going to do, I am going to write a cheque right now for a deposit." I didn't have the money for that cheque by the way, but I knew I had a credit card with space on it and I could get a cash advance and put the money into my account. "I am going to move into that house in two months and I am going to pay 10% of the purchase price down." I had no idea how that was going to come about. "Then I am going to pay an occupancy fee for 6 months and close the deal 6 months later."

The agent was like "WHAT?"

I said, "Well is it a legitimate offer?"

And he said, "Yeah I guess it is but I have never seen anything like it."

That idea just came to me. I didn't know how I was going to come up with the money. It filtered through my consciousness and I decided to just go with is. He wrote up the offer and went off to present it to Dr. John Goodman. I knew the cheque wouldn't be cashed till we had an agreed deal, so I ran to the bank and did a cash advance on my account to cover that cheque. He came back to me, and we negotiated a bit because I wanted all the furniture included, I wanted everything.

Then I went to Charles and asked if he was willing to keep the matrimonial home? I told him I was moving out. I said I had my own home, and I didn't need any of the furniture and he could keep it all. I was going to take my dishes and my clothes and our son's clothes. Charles didn't ask me what I was doing or how I was doing it. I don't think he really cared because he just wanted me gone and so he agreed to the deal.

Then I started freaking out. How in the world was I going to do this? This was a big old binding contract and I knew I had to follow through, I started feeling all this ugly stuff coming up inside of me, reverberating, like boiling bubbles. I had to talk myself down from the ledge.

"Stop. What is it that you would love?"

"I'd love to own that home."

"That all you have to focus on. You have manifested things before. This is no different from anything else you have manifested in the past."

So I calmed myself down and got myself centered and focused on what I wanted. I didn't tell anyone what I was doing. I told people I had bought a house. They didn't ask me where I got the money or how I was doing it or how was I able to buy a house when Charles was keeping our matrimonial home. I set my moving date. I had to come up with the 10% of the purchase price which was a significant amount of money and none of which I had.

I told a friend of mine about this, someone I could trust. She was positive, and a possibility thinker. After I'd explained what I'd done, she said, "Alright, well let's figure this out." She asked if I had any money in my re*TIR*ement account?

I was in my early 30s and I had put some money in years ago, but it was locked until I was 65. She thought there was a way I could take some of it out. I called the financial guy I had been dealing with years and asked about withdrawing my re*TIR*ement money.

He said, "Are you nuts? You'll pay penalties for it! That's for your retirement, Peggy. You're too young."

I told him that a home is an investment, and retirement money is an investment and there would plenty more for later. I was not concerned about that and I wanted to withdraw.

He got back to me and said if I took the money out in chunks, I'd be able to get the maximum amount which was exactly what I needed for the day I moved in - to the dollar! I withdrew the funds and then I had the money to move in and so we did.

Now I was in my dream home and no one knew that I had not closed the deal on the home. Nobody knew that I was paying an occupancy fee. When my friends came over to help me bring in my clothes and my dishes and my son's stuff the day I moved in they didn't know the circumstances around this deal. They were standing in this house wondering how I did it! It was a beautiful, spectacular home, full of upgrades and so beautifully done.

I was proudly walking around my home and feeling really good. Of course, it caused me to stretch. I had to get real creative. I had been working for this company that was in the internet space back in 1994, 1995 when the world wide web was just opening up. I happened to work for the first company in Canada to set up dedicated access to the world wide web which was unheard of at the time. People didn't even have websites yet. I was at the right place at the right time, but we create that, right? We manifest those right place, right time experiences.

This company I was working for decided to go public, and as an employee, I got to buy shares at very reduced rates from what they call the IPO, the initial public offering. I didn't know anything about the stock market or shares or anything, but they educated us as employees as to what we could expect.

Now my deal was closing on December 1st. I didn't have any money to close the deal on that house, but I committed that I was going to be closing on this house on December 1st. I figured I had 6 months to figure it out. So, I was living in the house and I was paying the occupancy fee. I'd paid the deposit on the house which was money I would lose if I didn't close the deal which was significant. I would be out on the street with my little boy. So I was in the home and all I had to do was focus on owning the home.

I started saving some money and I ended up putting all of that money on the stock in the company. It was a total gamble. It was like being at a roulette table and I put it all on one number, not knowing which way it was going to go. Whether the stock was going to go up, down or sideways, I had no idea.

The company was scheduled to go public in October. My house deal was closing on December 1st. I was feeling very anxious, and I would have moments of this choking feeling where I started thinking I was a fool and really doubted myself. I would have to stop myself from thinking these thoughts. I created these techniques so that when I felt that fear come up, I would just stop, get calm, take in a deep breath and ask, "Peggy, what would you love?"

"I would love to own this home."

"Great. So we are clear on that."

"What does it feel like now that you own this home?"

"Ahhh, it feels great."

"So what are you seeing in this home?"

"I am seeing us celebrate Christmas in the home."

I would create the vision of seeing us in the home for a long period of time, totally and fully enjoying the home. That would calm me down. The other thing I would do would be what's called vibrational alignment with the goods I desire. And I wouldn't do it once I would sometimes do it 37 times in a day because the fear would come up 37 times a day. I had to really work on that, kind of like conditioning: strengthening and strengthening.

I had put all the money I had saved on the company's stock, and as it was getting close to the day where the company was going to go public, they decided to move the IPO date. They were not ready yet so they moved it to November 26th.

I went to the broker and I asked, "Now the company is going to go public on November 26th and if I sell that day when do I get my money?"

The answer was four days later, which would be the 30th of November. I had hired a lawyer who said he needed the money for the transaction by the 30th of November, so we could close the deal on the 1st of December.

I assured him I would be in his office on the 30th with the money, but I still had no idea how I was going to do it. I had to see myself going to the lawyer's office to sign the papers. But I was totally freaking out inside and I had to really develop these methodologies of managing that emotion. I kept shifting or switching to what I wanted. When I saw myself heading toward a brick wall, I had to say 'No I don't want to go there'. I had switched over to where I wanted.

Well, the company went public on the 26th of November and the stock went skyrocketing. I sold it at its peak and had my money four days later. Champagne corks were popping on the first of December because I had a big party. I booked that party in advance with my friends and told them that I am having a party on December 1st and it was my house closing party.

It's like what Tony Robbins said in the video, it's not for what you get, it's for who you become. You've got to become very clear on what it is you want. I visualized owning that home before the draw, but what I should have been visualizing was winning the home. I should have visualized the phone call coming in from the GHEO foundation saying, "Peggy McColl, you won the home!" I should have seen the newspaper with my name and picture of me with the home. It's like Geneviève Behrend says, "Carefully examine the picture."

Carefully examine the picture, and in creating a picture, see a relaxed environment, not a totally stressed out choking, how the hell am I going to do this experience. Create clarity on that image.

There were periods of time I was starting to get images of my son and I with suitcases standing out on the street, and I would be thinking that's not going to happen, that's not going to happen. I also developed this healthy detachment, because even if it did happen I wouldn't be on the street. Charles would probably take us back in or my sister or my brother or my mother. I am not going to be out on the street.

You have to be willing to not be attached and I think that is where people get really challenged. They get attached and then have to detach themselves. I was talking to a client the other day who was telling me he is going through a divorce and he is a little freaked out. I asked what he was afraid of and he said he was afraid he wouldn't have any more money. I said, "What if that happened? There is plenty of abundance. Just go out and make some more. You made it before and you can make it again."

ॐ

Claudia DeVries

When I was 21 years old I left Surinam, my birth country and 'safe harbor' to go to Holland. There I wanted to become independent, study to become a teacher in hairdressing, and then go back to Surinam to start a hairdressing school.

Life had other plans for me: I fell madly in love with someone, so my plans to go back to Surinam completely changed when we decided to live together and make plans for the future.

However, things did not go the way I planned. My partner turned out to be extremely jealous, to a degree that I could not even talk to other men. If he was mad with me (and that was very often), he mentally abused me, making me feel like a zero. This was very new to me, and I did not know how to handle this because I was inexperienced in life as a whole.

That's when I got depressed (by that time I did not even know what that was). I could not go to work because I was crying the whole time, I slept on the cold floor in fetal posture, I did not want to eat and drink, I felt like I was drugged.

Then things got worse: we had to instantly leave the apartment that my partner was renting because it was in sublease. My partner simply left (he went to his father's house), leaving me alone to sleep on the street.

I did not know what to do. I was desperate. I went to the Housing Association for help. They could not give me any help because I did not live long enough in that city. At that moment it was too much to take. I could not hold my emotions any longer and I burst out in heavy tears. Someone saw that and promised to help me. He succeeded in getting me an apartment. Finally a bright spot in all those dark days!

But when I got the keys to the apartment, I could not believe my eyes. It was an extreme mess! The walls were torn apart, there was nothing left from the kitchen, there was no heating, the floors were extremely dirty and broken. Actually, everything was broken.

Apart from that, it was a very harsh winter and there was no heating at all. The windows had no double glass and I could feel a draft everywhere. Even though the situation was far from ideal I was grateful. Because... it was my own place!

But I had no idea how I was going to fix my situation. I was alone without any help in a foreign country. My parents and brothers all lived in Surinam. I did have some family in other cities, but I had no idea if they could or wanted to help me. I did not have much money, I was still weak from the depression, I was recovering from a broken heart, and the person that I had trusted and loved left me literally in the cold.

I tried to stay as calm as possible. In the very cold apartment, with many clothes on, and only a bedroom lamp, I prayed and began to make a plan to fix the apartment in the shortest time frame possible. I also prayed for somebody who could help me with very little payment.

I did find this wonderful person 2 days later. Somehow we did the job in less than 3 weeks, while all the work would surely take 3 months!

I was really happy and grateful for my apartment that I could call my own.

What I've learned from this lesson in life is to never give up hope, keep your faith, believe in yourself and always be persistent. And don't be afraid to let someone go who does not grow with you. You will always find someone else that will.

I did, and we are very happy together!

DANCING CAREER

When I was 26 years old I discovered Latin dancing. A new world opened for me. It looked so cool and I wanted to learn this! Soon I wanted to dance every evening. It became an addiction.

I came in contact with a Brazilian dance teacher who was the most popular Salsa teacher and dancer at the time. I wanted to learn to dance from him. But at one point, I did not just want to learn from him: I wanted to be his dance partner!

As I was not the youngest (26 years is quite 'old' in the dancing scene) and the best dancer at the time (imagine he was surrounded by a lot of talent and pretty ladies who were extremely willing to do the same), I decided to commit myself to train a lot and become very good. And that's exactly what I did!

Soon he began to notice me, and I was asked more often to assist him during lessons and trainings. When he got an interview in a video with Oscar D'León, he asked me to dance a demo with him. That became the beginning of my professional dance career as a Latin and Brazilian dancer. We performed a lot in Holland and abroad, and this was amazing. Never would I believe that this hobby would become my profession.

But... I wanted more than this. I wanted my own dance school.

This was not going to be easy. The Latin and Brazilian world at that time was a man's world, with many 'machos.' A colleague of mine also said to me when I told her what my goal was, "Claudia, our problem is that we are women." I did not accept this. I told her that although she saw it as a problem, I saw it as a big plus! And I would prove that too. I began to take action steps, and I truly believed that I would succeed with it. I would not give up. And I did not!

In two years' time, my dance school BraSaZouk was the biggest and most famous Latin and Brazilian dance school in Holland and Europe. It remained so for many years. Faith, action, and persistence had made this possible.

BIGGER GOAL

After successfully starting my own dance school at a location in Amsterdam in 2004, we had to move. The City Hall would restructure the area, and all buildings in that area were to be demolished. That was not pleasant at all! It would not be so easy to find another suitable location, but that is what we had to do.

In 2006, we found a place in an industrial area, where almost everything had to be built. Together with a business partner, I decided to go on this adventure.

Most people advised us not to do it: the place was too abandoned and dark, they suggested that it would not work, etc. We believed that it would succeed. In our imagination, we saw the studios already fully equipped and ready... crowded with musicians and dancers.

After the big renovation, it did seem like the people were right: we did not get clients, or at least not what we expected. People remained largely away for the first 2 years. But we continued to believe it would work. And it did so.

After 3 years, we began to reap the benefits of our hard work — until 2015 when, after just having finished a renovation at the location, we were faced with a special challenge: our studios went up in flames.

It seemed like a bad movie, but it was the hard reality. After we recovered from the shock of this nightmare and we got our feet down on earth again, we had to make choices. We were insured for calamities, but not insured enough. I was looking for a new location. It turned out to be a tiring and almost hopeless search because there were no suitable buildings or locations to get the studios back on track.

Eventually, we found a car showroom with a glass facade that could work well. Within 1 week I signed the lease agreement, and I could begin to apply for the right permits, to contract a building contractor, and to apply for loans at banks.

But... if I had known what challenges we were going to face, I probably would have thought twice about starting this new adventure. Or maybe not.

During construction, there were so many unforeseen costs that it made the entire cost twice as expensive! This meant that I had to borrow much more money than I had anticipated.

The banks, on the other hand, wanted to be sure that I would get all the necessary permits, so they did not want to grant the loans until I had them. However, I needed that money to pay the contractor in the meantime. Otherwise, he would stop the work.

The municipality did not want to release one of the most important licenses because an article had to be released by politics, a special procedure. So I had to meet certain conditions first. With great effort, I got that, and finally, everything started to flow.

I did have a big advantage during this tiring period, and that is that my partner is an architect and he designed the studios for me, delivering all the necessary drawings for the project in the fastest way he could, resulting in many nights of no sleep for him.

The contractor later stated that he did not think I would get it together to get all licenses and get all the money for the completion of the project. It was just not so simple to achieve that. In addition, he told me that what I asked for, to build everything in 3 months, was not possible. That would take at least 6 months. But I said it had to be done in 3 months and that it would succeed. And it did. I believed it would!

I must honestly say that during this whole process I did not have only positive emotions to get things done. The emotion I often had was anger, with which I did accomplish quite a few things. But I was exhausted from it. Anxiety did also play a part, but that brought me nothing. That's why I know that these emotions must definitely be omitted. Since I was so keen to succeed in doing this project, at the moment I did not even know which emotions often led me.

Anyways, after 3 months of sweat, tears, and hard labor, the new studios were a reality. Additionally, they were twice the size of the previous studios, and everything was in my own hands (without a business partner).

I now owned a beautiful location where all dance groups, dance schools, and dancers once again had a studio. And where happy, private parties and events can take place.

What I learned from this experience is that willpower and perseverance always yield fruit.

And if the desire is great, the goal will be achieved.

Monica DaMaren

My biggest story is the creation of my book using the power of auto-suggestion to develop my self-image and create what I wanted to become. I had a terrible self-image and did not believe I could write a best-selling book. It was too "out there" for me. I wasn't great in school, I wasn't great in English, and I was told I could never write a book.

I used the power of auto-suggestion and I applied the principles Bob taught me every day for six months. I set a goal to write and wrote my book within 7 weeks and self-published. During that time I used auto-suggestion. I used a journal to write every day 100 times, "I am an international best-selling author." I wrote the number of books I wanted to sell, and how many people I wanted to inspire. A lesson Bob teaches is to write your goal 100 times in the morning and at night and it will be burned into your subconscious. I really took that to heart. It's amazing what the universe will give you when you get in alignment with that frequency. You attract what you're in harmony with. At the beginning, I was only attracting what I was in harmony with, so I had to jump to those higher frequencies. Over time it didn't take long. I did mirror work and affirmations and visualization. After about a week I started believing I was going to become this person. There was no shadow of doubt in my mind. I started taking actions and steps that best-selling authors would take. People were coming into my life that I needed. I was having conversations with people that I needed to get me to my goal. Within 6 months on my launch date I became an international best-selling author and my book become number one in the USA and all of Canada in three hours.

It was my first big quantum leap. There were feelings and emotions I went through during my transformation. The best thing that happened was the person I became in the process.

When writing my goal in my journal, I had images cross my mind. I would see sales reports. I would see emails from readers all over the world saying, "Your book has changed my life and inspired me to live a better life myself." That was my drive so that is what I kept seeing. At first, it was such a little picture. But over time, every day and every week it kept getting clearer and clearer. Within a few weeks, I had a crystal-clear vision of where I wanted to go. During the six-month process I would tweak my process. I kept growing as a person and my dream kept getting bigger and more crystallized.

When I would close my eyes and visualize, at first it was a feeling. I would have a big smile on my face. I would have a feeling of fulfillment and happiness. That was great, as that was my Why and it had to be big. My next step was to change my self-image to match my Why. I would see myself becoming this successful, beautiful, happy, powerful woman. That's the image I would create in my mind. When I hooked onto my self-image, it all got connected.

Self-image is pretty powerful. Using visualization and auto-suggestion, as soon as self-image and self-confidence grow, that is the difference between someone being successful and not. Without it, you'll never achieve what you want.

Your self-image is a direct reflection of what you draw into your life. You can never out-perform your self-image, but you can change it. You can take goals and create freedom by changing your self-image. It's one of the most important things you have to change as you cannot attract outside your own self-image.

Whenever I set a goal I know I have to change my self-image to match that goal. Until I do I know I will not be able to attract the right people or things to my life to get me to that goal.

When you grow into your self-image that is when visualization becomes clear. Then you can attach emotions. Easy to close your eyes and picture something, but can you feel it? Visualization can be different for so many people.

It wasn't easy for me at the beginning. I had to practice. As I got into feeling my visualizations, the level was strengthened within myself and I was able to see the pictures.

I use visualization all the time. I've used visualization for other things as well. For example, I wanted to fly on Bob's private jet. I really wanted to get on that plane. All I had to do was ask of course, but I wanted him to ask me. And that's exactly how it went. He asked me to come on his plane to NYC to Carnegie Hall because they were honoring him. I was there with him to honor him, just like I had envisioned!

Ewa Pietrzak

The power of visualising — and how I've applied it to my goals.

When I worked in a full-time job as a financial analyst, over three years ago now, I had a strong desire to make changes in my personal and professional life. I wanted to give up finance and do what truly fulfilled me, but had no idea how to do it.

I had been following Bob Proctor online and decided to sign up to become a certified Proctor Gallagher Consultant.

I set myself a professional goal to leave my job and become a full-time entrepreneur and one way or another this was going to be my life and my business. At that stage I didn't know where I would get the money for my consultant fees, but I learned about the power of imagination and visualisation. After all, it had worked for the Wright brothers who invented airplanes and Edmund Hillary who was the first man to reach the top of Mount Everest, so I thought it may as well work for me.

So my path to becoming a consultant began with daily visualisations, using prompts like pictures and a vision board to help me see what I desired. I found pictures of women standing next to Bob Proctor and I pasted my face over theirs. I put those images on my vision board and I would look at them daily, seeing myself in Bob's inner circle of top performing consultants. (As of today, I've qualified for this six times in a row.)

On the way to my goal, one of my dreams was to attend the Matrixx event run by Bob and Sandy. Working in my full-time finance job in Dublin at the time, I had already borrowed funds to invest in consulting fees so I had no idea where the money would come from to travel to Toronto and pay for the highly priced Matrixx ticket as well. I placed my trust in the power of visualisation again and as if by magic, I got an invitation to be one of the event's facilitators. My event fees were all covered. This was proof of the power of imagining my goal despite the circumstances. According to Bob we are not meant to know how things will manifest, we just need to have faith they will. I always remember his line 'do your part by visualising your goal and allow the universe to do its amazing job'.

Once I've achieved my goal of being a full-time consultant, I set a big personal goal to attract my soulmate.

It was as important to me as building a successful and prosperous consulting business. I remember vividly a private meeting with Bob where other top consultants would ask him the secret of earning millions of dollars and I asked how to attract my partner. It was an unusual inquiry in that context but like with everything else, Bob was very clear and helpful.

He told me to write out all the personality traits and characteristics I desire in my partner and spend time daily visualising a person (without clear picture of his face) in my life. I took this to heart, as I truly wanted to have my partner to share my life with, and proceeded with daily visualisations. They had worked well for me already so every morning and night I would picture the same series of events: walking into my favourite restaurant in Dublin with my soulmate; our engaging conversation: what I was wearing and how he was dressed. I could even feel how he held my hand and smiled at me. Every evening I explored the picture in more and more details with all my senses, what I heard, saw, smelled, touched and most of all how I felt. I wanted a gentleman with great manners, and in my visualisations, he would open the door for me and put on my coat.

When the actual date happened a few months later, everything unfolded exactly as I practiced in my visualisation hundreds of times before, including him opening the door and putting on my coat. We are now happily engaged, and I will be forever grateful for Bob's guidance and the power of visualisation.

EWA'S TIPS

Many people ask me how they can implement the power of visualisation in their life. We do not have to visualise all parts of our goal but it's enough to create a scene or conversation that would happen once our goal manifests and go over it in detail at least twice a day for as long as the manifestation takes. When we do that we are creating a future memory and our mind believes it is actually happening. The mind is a masterful tool that always leads us to what we believe in, as it happened in the case of meeting my partner.

Start small, even two to five minutes in the morning and then just before bedtime. There are two mental faculties we need to develop in order to be very good at visualising. We need to train 'imagination' and 'will'.

If someone is completely new to this and has difficulty closing their eyes and picturing their goal, there is a very simple exercise that I highly recommend you do. Look at the palm of your hand and all the creases on it for a few minutes. Close your eyes and bring back the picture of your palm at the screen of your mind, as best as you can. If you do that simple activity every day for 30 days you're going to be able to picture things a lot quicker.

In order to train your intellectual faculty of 'will', which is also your ability to focus, try this exercise. Relax in your favourite chair, and light a candle right across from where you sit. You can also draw a dot on the wall or look at a painting. Then consciously bring your attention towards the dot or flame for 30-60 seconds and whenever your mind tries to wander, bring the attention back. Small exercises like this done consistently over a period of time strengthen your ability to visualise.

Another tip I would love to share will help you picture your dreams effectively. Focus on feelings experienced in your visualisation as if you have already achieved your goal. For example, you are sitting having that dinner with your soulmate or receiving an award on stage. What does it feel like? At first, I was very rigid about details when manifesting my partner. I focused on what he looked like and who he was, but this perfectionism disqualified many men from entering my life. Once I switched more into the emotional experience of what it 'feels' like to have that date in my favourite restaurant with someone who loves me, admires me and treats me like a queen, then, the feeling of my dream fulfilled settled in my mind much quicker and he showed up.

I also love playing emotional music while picturing my goals. It allows me to clear my mind and deepens the strength of visualisation. If you'd like to try this, look up 'epic emotional music' on YouTube and enjoy another level of picturing your goals.

Remember, you won't become an expert in a day so be patient with yourself. Start with few minutes right after waking up and just before bedtime and watch how the picture gets clearer and clearer and emotions increase. Pat yourself at the back for every progress you make and have fun with it.

Finally, if you'd love to shortcut your way to success, hire a mentor. As Bob Proctor says, having an expert showing you the way can save you up to 10 years of struggle and trying to figure it out your own way. I believe investing in my mentorship was the best investment I've ever made.

I use visualisation daily to run my busy consulting business helping hundreds of high achievers to fulfil their heart's desires. Whether it's setting up your own business, multiplying your income, attracting love, or shedding weight, I believe daily visualisation will hugely speed up the journey to achieving your goals.

ABOUT EWA

A success mentor and motivational speaker, Ewa Pietrzak offers webinars, events and powerful 24-week mentorship process, 'Thinking into Results'. Certified by Bob Proctor (*The Secret*), Ewa lives in Dublin and works with clients all over the world to help them get what they want in life.

If you loved our book and would like to get in touch, please connect with us on Facebook:

www.facebook.com/giahinternational/

If you are interested in finding out more about our course Visualization to Realization and/or The Proctor Gallagher Institute "Thinking into Results" or the "Matrixx" please do not hesitate to contact us at:

jackie@giahinternational.com

We sincerely wish for you a brilliant life, one that you are madly in love with. We get one life, one shot, let's make it a damn good one!

> *"Live with a dream in your head, hope in your heart and smile on your face!"*
>
> ~ *Jackie Carroll*

Printed in Great Britain
by Amazon